HUNTER DAVIES

Some fairly interesting things about
Hunter Davies:

1 Has no grey hair, even at his age
2 Writes a terrific column in *Stamp and
   Postal History News*
3 And also a very good one in *Punch*
   called 'Father's Day'
4 Has three children, not all of them
   speaking to him at the moment
5 Has had two cartilage operations but
   thinks he can still play Sunday morning
   football
6 Was born in Johnstone, Scotland, in . . .
   ok, if you insist . . . 1936
7 Brought up in Carlisle
8 Has written 20 books
9 His biographies include The Beatles,
   William Wordsworth, George
   Stephenson and the Grades
10 Is terribly fond of walking round Great
   Britain
11 Wrote the novel and film *Here We Go,
   Round the Mulberry Bush*
12 Collects stamps, postcards, Lake District
   books, American railway bonds, Beatle
   memorabilia and, of course, lists.

GEORGE DARBY

A few fairly boring things about
George Darby:

1 Has many grey hairs, even at an age
   less than that of H. Davies Esq.
2 Holds down a responsible job on the
   Sunday Times instead of writing terrific
   columns
3 Puts grey hairs down to employing
   people such as H. Davies
4 Has four children, all of them speaking –
   if only to themselves
5 Was born in Bolton, Lancashire, in
   (proudly) 1942 – the town that also begat
   Nat Lofthouse, Jack Hylton and
   Ian McKellan
6 Has written about eight books, mostly
   ghosted, on folk ranging from John
   Bloom to snooker superchamp Joe
   Davis, and edits *The Sunday Times
   Bedside Book*
7 Used to be a member of the National
   Youth Orchestra of Great Britain, and
   played the oboe – 'an ill wind that
   nobody blows good'
8 Is terribly fond of Bolton Wanderers,
   the only living person to suffer such an
   affliction
9 Is attending Chelsea matches as a cure,
   but to little avail
10 Collects original cartoons, American
   Express accounts and, of course, lists
11 Can't think of anything – even dull –
   after number 10
12 Does that mean Carlisle United beats
   Bolton Wanderer 12–10?

HUNTER DAVIES'S BIGGER BOOK OF BRITISH LISTS

Edited by Hunter Davies
and George Darby

Hamlyn Paperbacks

HUNTER DAVIES'S BIGGER BOOK OF BRITISH LISTS
ISBN 0 600 20480 4

First published in Great Britain 1982
by Hamlyn Paperbacks
Copyright © 1982 by Hunter Davies

Hamlyn Paperbacks are published by
The Hamlyn Publishing Group Ltd,
Astronaut House
Feltham
Middlesex, England

Reproduced, printed and bound in Great Britain by
Hazell Watson & Viney Ltd, Aylesbury, Bucks

CONTENTS

IRELAND

SCOTLAND

WALES

ACKNOWLEDGEMENTS

We would like to thank the researchers for all their work in the preparation of this book. They are:

Barbara Gilgallon
Ian Marter
Nicholas Mason
Sue Seddon
David Thomas
Liz Davies (Wales)
Liam McAuley (Ireland)
Jack Webster (Scotland)

Additional research:
Paul Donnelley

We would also like to thank all the authors, editors and publishers of the publications mentioned.

Introduction

We got an enormous response from our first *Book of British Lists*. The reaction really was overwhelming. But despite all that, we decided to do another . . .

No, it genuinely was a success, getting straight on to the best-seller list, which of course is where all books of lists should be. Terry Wogan, the well-known man of letters, was kind enough to welcome it as: 'Riveting trivia – one of the most stimulatingly useless books I've ever read. I loved every page of it . . .' It proved very popular with a wide cross-section of the Great British public. After all, it was for and about them.

So many people sent in lists they had done themselves, or were prompted into making their own lists when they saw the ones we had compiled, that we just had to do another book.

The first book, published back in 1980 and running into several editions and reprints, was begun through a real interest in lists on any subject, from shopping lists to Government statistics. In all the non-fiction books I have written, which I like to think are real books, as opposed to list books, which are written in the margins of life to be read in the margins of life, I have always thrown in lots of lists at the end, the stuff I haven't been able to work in, though naturally I have called them Appendices. These have often caused more correspondence, and more interest, than the books themselves.

The other reason for doing that first book was as an answer to an American book of lists, full of lists about American life and culture, which was then on sale in Great Britain. Our book might be rubbish, so we thought, but at least it would be British rubbish.

The *Bigger Book of British Lists* is not only completely new, and bigger, and naturally very much better now that we've got the hang of these things, but something strange has happened. It's not so trivial. However, there are still a large number of daft and dopey lists which I am sure you will enjoy, such as the list of answers to his letters which a fifteen-year-old schoolboy compiled after writing to famous people asking them to speak at his school (see under L for Letters). I also like the unemployed law graduate's list of all the stupid prizes he has won in radio competitions about pop music (see Q for Quiz).

These are just two of the unsolicited lists which were sent in by readers of the first book.

That first book was very much my own bit of cottage industry, doing most of the research myself, with the aid of my children and friends. Now Hamlyn's, carried away with dreams of avarice, have spent money on professional researchers, and we have been able to employ some very well-known journalists and writers. Don't just feel the length. Admire the quality.

In that first book, we were rather oriented towards London and the South, a feature of so many books which pretend they are about 'Great Britain'. It's understandable, as that's where the biggest conurbation is, and where most book writers do their book writing, but it is often a pity.

So, in the *Bigger Book of British Lists*, we have created three separate sections devoted to Ireland (North and South), Scotland and Wales, setting suitable natives to select the lists. Through their own choice of subjects you get an insight into the national characteristics. All Irish, Scots and Welsh should find these sections of interest, even the ones living in London and the South, which of course is where millions of Irish, Scots and Welsh now live. (Speaking as two of them. Yup, born in Scotland, with a Welsh surname, though brought up in the North of England, now living in London. Thank you.)

I hope you will find this book as amusing as the first one, and as interesting and original, but beware, another element has crept in. You might actually *learn* something this time. However, it shouldn't harm your health.

From now on you will be able to show off for hours with your newly-acquired knowledge of the rude words which are not allowed in the House of Commons, or bore your friend across the room as you read out a list of famous British homosexuals from this book as it lies on the counter – and if you *are* doing that, then stop it at once and pay for it. Bloody cheek.

Once again, it has been fun to compile and edit and, so we all hope, fun to read. If the response is again phenomenal then, you never know, we might be forced to bow to public pressure. If you have a list, then list it, as we are all now feeling decidedly listless.

Hunter Davies
London, February 1982

A's

We couldn't begin with something depressing, such as abortions or accidents, so we cheated and opened the London Telephone Directory and wrote down the first ten surnames of real people beginning with the letter A. Goodness, this book is going to be easy to write. Guess what sort of list we have under the letter Z?

The first ten names in the London telephone directory

Aabelton
Aafili
Aalam
Aalberg
Aalders

Aalen
Aamer
Aan de wiel
Aanonson
Aapavaara

ABORTION

Most gynaecologists will say that there are as many different reasons for requesting an abortion as there are women who have abortions. However, it is possible to list the most common reasons given in Britain over the past few years:

Inability to cope financially with a child at present
Too young or too old to cope with a child
Unable to cope emotionally with pregnancy and birth
Family now completed
Need to continue studies or career
Pressure from partner or relatives
Relationship with the father ended through desertion or death
Medical reasons
Fear that the child would be deformed
Pregnancy the result of a purely accidental or casual relationship

ACCIDENTS AT WORK

Health and Safety Executive, Social Trends

type of industry	accidents	fatal accidents
Manufacturing	133 164	125
Coal-mining	36 758	42
Construction	29 492	128
Railways	4 391	30
Quarrying	—	17
Agriculture	4 248	24

Although there were 125 fatal accidents in manufacturing industry in 1980, this represents a rate of only 3 per 100 000 workers. The rate for the coal-mining industry was much higher – 15 per 100 000.

A QUESTION
(the answer to which comes under the letter A)

Where on earth would you find the following places?

Ambition Room
Assembly of Ancestors
Fourth Gutter
Insect Ditch
Jade Pillow
Leg Three Miles
Little Rushing In

Not At Ease
One Hundred Meetings
Palace Of Weariness
People Welcome
Receive Tears
Suspended Pivot
Walking On The Verandah

You'd find them all somewhere on your own body. They are the names of *acupuncture* points.

ADVERTISING

Top ten advertising agencies, 1981

Campaign Magazine

billings in £ millions 1981	agency	billings in £ millions 1980	position in 1981
101.20	Saatchi and Saatchi Garland Compton	83.00	}1
96.10	J. Walter Thompson	83.00	}1
88.00	D'Arcy MacManus and Masius	75.00	}3
76.54	McCann Erickson Advertising	75.00	}3
71.40	Ogilvy Benson and Mather	61.20	5
60.69	Collett Dickenson Pearce	60.89	6
56.00	Foote Cone and Belding	45.22	8
52.36	Young and Rubicam	46.41	7
50.32	Allen Brady and March	39.12	10
46.00	Dorland Advertising	38.00	11

Some favourite advertisements

Peter Marsh, the flamboyant chairman of advertising agency Allen Brady and Marsh, is the man responsible for the Wonder of Woolworths and the Age of the Train. Here are his eight favourite advertisements of all time.

1　The Badedas press advertisement – 'Things happen after a Badedas bath' – featuring a woman looking out over a lawn on which a helicopter stands.
2　The Cyril Lord television advertisement for Enkalon carpets; the first ABM television commercial. Sadly, Cyril ended up broke.
3　The Volkswagen 'snow-plough' ad, an American advertisement that asked the brilliant question, 'How does the driver of the snow-plough reach it when all the roads are snowed under?' The answer was that he drove a Volkswagen.
4　The Imperial Leather advertisement that featured a couple and their son relaxing in triple baths. This gave an impression of immense luxury that was compounded by the fact that they all turned out to have been bathing in an aeroplane.

5 The Smash Martians TV commercial.
6 The press campaign mounted by the Bristol Channel Ship Repairers anti-nationalization protest.
7 The press advertising for Clark's shoes in the winter of 1977/78.
8 The hair gel advertisement that claimed, 'Friday night is Amami night'.

ADVISORY AND COUNSELLING SERVICES

National Consumer Council

The following figures are for 1980.

	centres	volunteer helpers	clients
Citizens' Advice Bureaux	879	12 000	4 367 100
Law centres	30	500	96 000
Young People's Counselling and Advisory Service	55	200	30 000
Catholic Marriage Advisory Service	68	400	3 200
Marriage Guidance Council	176	2 900	36 700
Alcoholics Anonymous	1465	NA	25 000
Samaritans	168	19 800	298 600

ALCOHOLICS

Either dead or reformed.

1 Donald Maclean (spy)
2 Guy Burgess (spy)
3 Sarah Churchill (actress)
4 Jimmy Greaves (footballer)
5 George Best (footballer)
6 Dylan Thomas (poet)
7 Edward VIII (later the Duke of Windsor)
8 Brendan Behan (writer)
9 Scott Fitzgerald (writer)

ATHLETICS

Four minutes and faster . . . and faster . . .

The world mile record has been lowered 14 times since Roger Bannister's epic run at Oxford in 1954. This is how it has been done:

3 min 59.4 sec	Roger Bannister	(Great Britain)	6 May 1954
3 min 57.9 sec	John Landy	(Australia)	21 June 1954
3 min 57.2 sec	Derek Ibbotson	(Great Britain)	19 July 1957
3 min 54.5 sec	Herb Elliott	(Australia)	6 August 1958
3 min 54.1 sec	Peter Snell	(New Zealand)	27 January 1962
3 min 53.6 sec	Michel Jazy	(France)	9 June 1965
3 min 51.3 sec	Jim Ryun	(USA)	17 July 1966
3 min 51.1 sec	Jim Ryun	(USA)	23 June 1967
3 min 51.0 sec	Filbert Bayi	(Tanzania)	17 May 1975
3 min 49.4 sec	John Walker	(New Zealand)	12 August 1975
3 min 49.0 sec	Sebastian Coe	(Great Britain)	17 July 1979
3 min 48.8 sec	Steve Ovett	(Great Britain)	1 July 1980
3 min 48.53 sec	Sebastian Coe	(Great Britain)	19 August 1981
3 min 48.40 sec	Steve Ovett	(Great Britain)	26 August 1981
3 min 47.33 sec	Sebastian Coe	(Great Britain)	28 August 1981

The Marathon

Not further, but faster . . . Though no Briton has won an Olympic marathon title, Britain's tradition in that most formidable of all road races is long and distinguished. The very length of the race – 26 miles 385 yards – was the distance laid down for the London Olympic Games Marathon of 1908, and it has remained the same ever since. This is the way the times have improved for British runners since the statutory distance was established (in hrs/mins/secs).

time	runner	venue	date
2:42.31	Fred Barrett*	Windsor–Stamford Bridge	26 May 1909
2:38.17	Harry Green*	Shepherd's Bush	12 May 1913
2:37.41	Arthur Mills	Windsor–Stamford Bridge	17 July 1920
2:35.59	Sam Ferris	Windsor–Stamford Bridge	30 May 1925
2:35.27	Sam Ferris	Liverpool	28 September 1927
2:34.34	Harry Payne	Windsor–Stamford Bridge	6 July 1928

2:33.00	Sam Ferris	Liverpool	26 September 1928
2:30.58	Harry Payne	Windsor–Stamford Bridge	5 July 1929
2:29.28	Jim Peters	Windsor–Chiswick	16 June 1951
2:20.43	Jim Peters*	Windsor–Chiswick	14 June 1952
2:18.41	Jim Peters*	Windsor–Chiswick	13 June 1953
2:18.35	Jim Peters*	Turku, Finland	4 October 1953
2:17.40	Jim Peters*	Windsor–Chiswick	26 June 1954
2:14.43	Brian Kilby	Port Talbot	6 July 1963
2:13.55	Basil Heatley*	Windsor–Chiswick	13 June 1964
2:13.45	Alastair Wood	Inverness–Forres	9 July 1966
2:12.17	Bill Adcocks	Karl Marx Stadt, E. Germany	19 May 1968
2:10.48	Bill Adcocks	Fukuoka, Japan	8 December 1968
2:10.30	Ron Hill	Boston, Mass., USA	20 April 1970
2:09.28	Ron Hill	Edinburgh	23 July 1970
2:09.12	Ian Thompson	Christchurch, New Zealand	31 January 1974

* also a world's best time.

AUTHORS

The Book Marketing Council, in a brave attempt to push British books, did a special promotion in 1982. They drew up a list of twenty top authors and mounted displays of their books in around 4000 British bookshops.

They started with 100 names, submitted by publishers, and then whittled them down. Quite a few oldies crept in. Quite a few equally distinguished authors were omitted. Where was Angus Wilson, Kingsley Amis?

The BMC quickly added that it was not *the* Top Twenty but *a* Top Twenty.

Best of British Authors, 1982

Beryl Bainbridge
John Betjeman
Malcolm Bradbury
Anthony Burgess
Margaret Drabble
Lawrence Durrell
John Fowles
Leon Garfield
William Golding
Graham Greene

Ted Hughes
John Le Carré
Laurie Lee
Rosamond Lehmann
Iris Murdoch
V. S. Naipaul
V. S. Pritchett
Rosemary Sutcliffe
Laurens Van Der Post
Rebecca West

AUTOBIOGRAPHIES

Why not try out on your friends the following list of titles and see if they can guess the author?

It will be easy for you. You're looking at the answers. This list, by the way, is one of several compiled by Paul Donnelley of Harold Hill, Essex, who read and was amazed by our first *Book of British Lists* and has been busy creating his own lists ever since. Thank you, Paul.

1	Prof Keith Simpson	*40 Years of Murder*
2	Prof R. V. Jones	*Most Secret War*
3	Jimmy Greaves	*This One's On Me*
4	Norris McWhirter	*Ross: Story of a Shared Life*
5	Oliver Reed	*Reed All About Me*
6	Robert Graves	*Goodbye to All That*
7	Colin Cowdrey	*M.C.C.*
8	Stewart Grainger	*Sparks Fly Upwards*
9	Jim Watt	*Watt's My Name*
10	Joey Deacon	*Tongue-Tied*
11	Doris Stokes	*Voices in My Ear*
12	Robert Dougall	*In and Out of the Box*
13	Reginald Bosanquet	*Let's Get Through Wednesday*
14	David Jacobs	*Jacob's Ladder*
15	Dame Vera Lynn	*Vocal Refrain*
16	Des O'Connor	*Somebody Laughed*
17	Jimmy Savile	*As It Happens*
18	Peter Ustinov	*Dear Me*
19	Sir John Gielgud	*Early Stages*
20	Jack Warner	*Evening All*

BANKRUPTCY

Numbers of company failures classified by trade, 1980

Dept of Trade, Report for the year 1980

Construction	780
Food retailers	293
Other retailers	273
Road haulage/taxi hire	272
Restaurants, pubs and clubs	223
Garages, motor dealers, filling stations	192
Financial/business/professional services	192
Other consumer services	145
Manufacturing	127

So the construction industry wins. In 1980, it represented a total deficiency of about £5 million – on average about £6578 per case. There were three cases of liabilities of over £1 million.

Signs to look out for . . .

William Mackay, who was the Receiver called in by Laker, suggests that if your company has three or more of the following you could have problems coming soon:

1 Rolls Royce with personalized number plates
2 Fish tank or fountain in the reception area
3 Flag pole
4 Queen's Award for Industry (UK only)
5 Chairman honoured for services to industry
6 Salesman or engineer as chief executive
7 Recently moved to modern offices
8 Unqualified or elderly accountant
9 Products a market leader
10 Recently changed bankers
11 Audit partner who grew up with the company

12 Chairman a politician or well known for his charitable works
13 Announced huge order for Afghanistan
14 Satisfied personnel with no strike record
15 Recently announced a technical breakthrough

BEAUTY

Miss United Kingdom

1972 Jenny McAdam (London)
1973 Veronica Cross (London)
1974 Helen Morgan (Barry)
1975 Vicki Harris (London)
1976 Carol Grand (Glasgow)
1977 Madeleine Stringer (North Shields)
1978 Ann Jones (Welshpool)
1979 Carolyn Seaward (Plymouth)
1980 Kim Ashfield (Clwyd)
1981 Tracey Dodds (Sheffield)

Miss World

1972 Belinda Green (Australia)
1973 Marji Wallace (USA)
1974 Helen Morgan (UK – resigned)
     Anneline Kriel (South Africa)
1975 Wilnelia Merced (Puerto Rico)
1976 Cindy Breakspeare (Jamaica)
1977 Mary Stavin (Sweden)
1978 Silvana Suarez (Argentina)
1979 Gina Swainson (Bermuda)
1980 Kimberley Santos (Guam)
1981 Pilin Leon (Venezuela)

BED

After beauty, then we naturally come to bed – alphabetically speaking, of course. According to a Gallup survey in 1981, Britons now spend less time in bed than in 1958.

Bed-time habits

16% of adults are up by 6.30 a.m. compared with 1% in 1958

14% of adults are still up after midnight compared with 2% in 1958

50% of the population sleep with a window open even in winter

41% of men and 17% of women sleep naked (except in Scotland)

33% of Britons sleep under a Duvet (40% in Scotland)

Once in bed, about a third of the population goes straight to sleep, and of the remainder:

40% read books
17% listen to the radio
17% read newspapers or magazines
 5% listen to records

and only 7% admit to doing 'the usual things' . . .

BIRDS
Endangered species
Royal Society for the Protection of Birds

Many species of bird have become rare and even in danger of disappearing from Britain altogether as a result of climatic changes, pollution, hunting, egg-stealing. Among them are the following (in alphabetical order):

Dartford Warbler Reduced to perhaps only 12 breeding pairs in 1963 as a result of severe winter and progressive destruction of heathland habitats. Gradual revival. In 1974 about 560 pairs were recorded.

Golden Eagle Constantly declining population particularly due to deliberate poisoning by farmers. Now about 300 breeding pairs.

Marsh Harrier Driven from its East Anglian haunts by increasing numbers of holidaymakers and by the Coypu (a species of water rat). About 20 breeding pairs at the last count.

Osprey By 1900 the bird had been shot out of Britain. In the mid-50s it had begun to reappear and 20 pairs were counted.

Peregrine Falcon A victim of agricultural pesticides. Now perhaps 450 pairs.

Redbacked Shrike Progressively rarer – 300 pairs were breeding in 1952 but only 80 or 90 by 1971 as a result of egg-stealing. Today there may be fewer than 50 pairs.

Red Kite As commonplace in medieval London streets as pigeons are today. Human disturbance, egg stealing and poison have reduced it to 30 breeding pairs confined to the Welsh hills.

White-tailed Eagle or **Sea Eagle** Relentlessly hunted until it died out completely early this century. Gradually re-introduced from Scandinavia to the Hebridean Island of Rhum at the rate of 25 birds a year.

BLOOMING BRITAIN

Winners of *Britain in Bloom* – an annual competition sponsored by the British Tourist Authority

year	city	town	village
1971	Aberdeen	Falmouth	Abington, Strathclyde
1972	Bath Hartlepool	Ayr	Chagford, Devon
1973	Aberdeen	Bridlington Falmouth	Ryton, Tyne and Wear

1974	Aberdeen City of London		Shrewsbury	Clovelly, Devon
1975	Bath		Sidmouth	Clovelly, Devon
1976	Bath		Harrogate	Bampton, Devon
1977	Aberdeen		Harrogate	Wolviston, Cleveland
1978	Bath	*large*	Douglas	Aberdovey, Gwynedd
		small	Sidmouth	Carrington, Lothian
1979	Aberdeen	*large*	Harrogate	Holywell, Northumberland
		small	Falmouth St Andrews	
1980	Exeter	*large*	Douglas	Killingworth, Tyne and Wear
		small	Ryton	
1981	Bath	*large*	Harrogate	Pateley Bridge, Yorkshire
		small	Sidmouth	St John's Town of Dalry, Dumfries and Galloway

THE BLUE PLAQUE GUIDE TO LONDON

There are 427 blue plaques on London houses, commemorating the fact that some famous person once lived there. Here are ten fascinating facts about them, gathered by Caroline Dakers:

1 **Charles Dickens,** the person with the most plaques.

Charles Dickens has six plaques commemorating houses (and sites of houses) in which he lived in London, ranging from his deprived childhood in Camden Town to his last and grandest London home, Tavistock House in Bloomsbury. The house at 48 Doughty Street where he wrote *Oliver Twist* and *Nicholas Nickleby* is now a museum and open to the public.

2 **Lord Brockway** (pacifist Fenner Brockway), the only living person to have a plaque.

The London Borough of Islington have erected a plaque on one of the earliest of his homes at 60 Myddelton Square.

3　**John Dryden,** commemorated by the oldest plaque.

In 1875 the Royal Society of Arts commemorated the poet John Dryden's home in Gerrard Street, Soho. Unfortunately the plaque was placed on the wrong house, number 43 instead of number 44.

4　**Fryderyk Chopin,** commemorated by one of the most recent plaques.

While Chopin was staying at 4 St James's Place for a month in 1848 he gave the last public concert of his life at the Guildhall, in aid of Polish refugees.

5　**Colen Campbell** and **Sir John Vanbrugh,** two architects commemorated by plaques on houses they built for themselves.

Colen Campbell, the architect of Stourhead, Wiltshire, built his own house at 76 Brook Street in 1726. Vanbrugh, soldier, dramatist and architect of Castle Howard and Blenheim Palace, built a castle for himself on Maze Hill, Greenwich in 1717.

6　**R. Norman Shaw,** the architect, commemorated by a plaque on a house he built for someone else.

'Grimsdyke' in the Harrow Weald was designed by Norman Shaw in the 'Old English' style for the painter Frederick Goodall, who filled the grounds with Egyptian sheep. A later resident, W. S. Gilbert, drowned while attempting to save a female guest bathing in the lake.

7　**Thomas De Quincey,** the writer with the wrongly spelt plaque.

Thomas De Quincey's name appears as Quincy on the house at 36 Tavistock Street, Covent Garden, where he wrote his *Confessions of an English Opium-Eater*.

8　**Lillie Langtry,** the actress with the wrong date of birth on her plaque.

The 'Jersey Lily' and mistress of the Prince of Wales was born in 1853 and not, as her plaque on the Cadogan Hotel states, in 1852.

9　**Dame Joanna Astley,** one of the most obscure recipients of a plaque.

Dame Joanna was nurse to the young Henry VI,

receiving a salary of £40 a year. St Bartholomew's Hospital now covers the site of her home.

10 **Thomas Chatterton, Lord Clive of India** and **Sir Samuel Romilly,** three men who committed suicide in their houses, each of which is commemorated with a plaque.

Lonely, starving and poverty-stricken, the eighteen-year-old poet Chatterton swallowed arsenic in his lodgings in Brooke Street, Holborn in 1770. Lord Clive took an overdose of laudanum at his home, 45 Berkeley Square, in 1774. Sir Samuel Romilly, law-reformer and supporter of the freedom of slaves, killed himself at his home, 21 Russell Square, a few days after the death of his wife in 1818.

BOOKS
British book titles, 1981
The Bookseller

The number of titles published in 1981 was 43,083. Fiction topped the list of subjects.

Top Twenty Categories

Fiction	4747
Political science and economy	3764
Children's books	2934
Medical science	2838
School textbooks	1991
Engineering	1488
History	1432
Law and public administration	1399
Art	1383
Religion and theology	1363
Biography	1243
Natural sciences	1234
Commerce	1213
Literature	1151

Education	1040
Sociology	1031
Bibliography and library economy	788
Mathematics	726
Psychology	725
Domestic science	695

Commerce has dropped from tenth place in 1980 to thirteenth. Chemistry and physics has dropped altogether from the Top Twenty after holding seventeenth place in 1980. Newcomer Domestic science just scrapes into twentieth position vacated by ascendant Mathematics, now in eighteenth position. Engineering has ousted Religion and theology which plummets four places to finish between Art and Biography.

Growth in book sales 1947–80

The Bookseller

year	total	year	total
1947	13 046	1964	26 154
1948	14 686	1965	26 358
1949	17 034	1966	28 883
1950	17 072	1967	29 619
1951	18 066	1968	31 470
1952	18 741	1969	32 393
1953	18 257	1970	33 489
1954	18 188	1971	32 538
1955	19 962	1972	33 140
1956	19 107	1973	35 254
1957	20 719	1974	32 194
1958	22 143	1975	35 608
1959	20 690	1976	34 434
1960	23 783	1977	36 322
1961	24 893	1978	38 766
1962	25 079	1979	41 940
1963	26 023	1980	48 158

The number of titles published in 1981 (43,083) shows a substantial fall for the first time.

Best sellers, 1981

The following are the best-selling hardback books of 1981, based on appearances in the weekly best-seller lists published in the *Sunday Times* newspaper, and specially analyzed by Pat Hartridge.

NON-FICTION

The Guinness Book of Records (Guinness Superlatives) headed the *Sunday Times* non-fiction list nine times following its publication on 1 November, 1981

The Lord God Made Them All by James Herriot (Michael Joseph) stayed at Number 1 for seven weeks and then made a further fifteen appearances

Invitation to a Royal Wedding by Kathleen Spink (Colour Library International) topped the list for five weeks and finished the year at Number 2 after reaching the top ten another seventeen times

Ireland: a History by Robert Kee (Weidenfeld) stayed at the top for five weeks. Based on the successful TV series

James Herriot's Yorkshire, with photographs by Derry Brabbs (Michael Joseph) started 1981 in first place and notched up forty appearances during the year, totalling 184 since publication in late 1979

The Country Diary of an Edwardian Lady by Edith Holden (Webb & Bower/Michael Joseph) retired from the listings in March 1981 after achieving 184 entries since 1978

FICTION

Rites of Passage by William Golding (Faber). Winner of the 1980 Booker Prize, it headed the league for eight weeks at the end of that year and remained at the top for another ten weeks in 1981

Noble House by James Clavell (Hodder) topped the Fiction listing thirteen times in 1981

Twice Shy by Dick Francis (Michael Joseph) and *X.P.D.* by Len Deighton (Hutchinson) both reached Number 1 for six weeks during the year

Midnight's Children by Salman Rushdie (Cape) was the 1981

Booker Prizewinner and it ended the year by heading the list twice.

Michael Joseph achieve something of a publishing coup with no less than four titles in the above lists. No other publisher manages more than one.

Best-selling paperbacks, 1981

The Bookseller

Although it was Royal Wedding year, the wedding titles – such as *Not! The Royal Wedding* – were all outsold by the various books about Rubik's Cube from Puffin and Corgi. A year bristling with film and television tie-ins ended with *The French Lieutenant's Woman* and *Brideshead Revisited* dominating the heights.

The Top Twenty Paperbacks were all fiction titles:

Tilly Trotter by Catherine Cookson (Corgi)	539 000
Kane and Abel by Jeffrey Archer (Coronet)	463 000
A Falcon Flies by Wilbur Smith (Pan)	363 000
If There Be Thorns by Virginia Andrews (Fontana)	363 000
Princess Daisy by Judith Krantz (Corgi)	336 000
The Bourne Identity by Robert Ludlum (Granada)	296 000
Athabasca by Alistair Maclean (Fontana)	286 000
Solo by Jack Higgins (Fontana)	285 000
Smiley's People by John Le Carré (Pan)	281 000
The Jonah by James Herbert (New English Library)	280 000
To Love Again by Danielle Steel (Sphere)	265 000
The French Lieutenant's Woman by John Fowles (Granada)	256 000
Random Winds by Belva Plain (Fontana)	236 000
The Wilt Alternative by Tom Sharpe (Pan)	235 000
A Woman of Substance by Bradford Taylor (Granada)	230 000
The Flowers of the Field by Sarah Harrison (Futura)	222 000
Brideshead Revisited by Evelyn Waugh (Penguin)	215 000
A Rage of Angels by Sidney Sheldon (Pan)	200 000
Sins of the Father by Susan Howatch (Pan)	196 000
Duncton Wood by William Horwood (Hamlyn)	196 000

The above figures include 1981 Home Sales only.

Children's best sellers, 1981

National Book League

Including both paperback and hardback titles:

H.R.H. The Prince of Wales by Ian Morrison (Ladybird)
Grange Hill Goes Wild by Robert Leeson (Fontana)
The Royal Wedding by Audrey Daly (Ladybird)
Where's Spot? by Eric Hill (Heinemann)
You Can Do The Cube by Patrick Bossert (Puffin)
The Old Man Of Lochnagar by H.R.H. The Prince of Wales (Hamish Hamilton)
Robot by Jan Pienkowski (Heinemann)
The Most Amazing Hide And Seek Counting Book by Robert Crowther (Kestrel)
The End by Richard Stanley (Puffin)
The Patchwork Cat by William Mayne and Nicola Bayley (Cape)

Oddest book titles

Bruce Robertson of the Diagram Group has been collecting odd book titles at the Frankfurt Book Fair for over ten years. Here is the shortlist of oddest titles for 1981, headed by the winner:

Last Chance at Love – Terminal Romances
Child-Spacing in Tropical Africa
Physical Properties of Slags
A Pictorial Book of Tongue-Coatings
The Power of Positive Intimidation in Selling
The Bio-Chemist's Song-Book
The Gray's Anatomy Colouring Book
A Frog's Blimp
Fifty New Poodle Grooming Styles
New Guinea Tapeworms and Jewish Grandmothers
Cats' Revenge: More than 101 Uses for Dead People
Children Are Like Wet Cement

Seven Years of 'Manifold': 1968–1980
Short-Term Visual Information Forgetting
Waterproofing Your Child

The winner in 1980 was *The Joy of Chickens*.

BOXING
Britain's champions

We've not got a lot to go on about but the following Britons have all held the title of world champion at their respective weights:

Heavyweight
Bob Fitzsimmons   1897–99

Light Heavyweight
Bob Fitzsimmons   1903–05
Freddie Mills   1948–50
John Conteh*   1974–77

Middleweight
Bob Fitzsimmons   1891–97
Randolph Turpin   1951
Terry Downes   1961–62
Alan Minter   1980

Light Middleweight
Maurice Hope*   1979–81

Welterweight
Matt Wells   1914–15
Ted 'Kid' Lewis   1915–16, 1917–19
John H. Stracey   1975–76

Light Welterweight
Jack 'Kid' Berg   1930–31

Lightweight
Freddie Welsh   1915–17
Ken Buchanan   1970–72
Jim Watt*   1979–81

Featherweight
Howard Winstone**   1968

Bantamweight
Joe Bowker   1904–05

Flyweight
Jimmy Wilde   1916–23
Jackie Brown   1932–35
Benny Lynch   1935, 1937–38
Peter Kane   1938–43
Jackie Paterson   1943–48
Rinty Monaghan   1948–50
Terry Allen   1950
Walter McGowan   1966

* Recognized as champion by World Boxing Council
** Recognized as 'British World Champion'

A number of claimants not recognized as champions outside
Britain and Europe have not been included.

CALORIES IN FAST FOODS
Arline Usden: In Great Shape

Does fast food make you fat fast? Should you fast first? Do we
need to eat for heat? Forget the questions. Let's just have the
facts . . .

1 piece crispy chicken	225	taramasalata	315
small portion chips	270	doner kebab	650
coleslaw	100	3 stuffed vine leaves	170
barbecued beans	100	lamb kebabs	360
	695	Greek salad	100

¼ pound hamburger	420	beef curry and rice	875–1000
small french fries	210	vegetable curry	270
chocolate milkshake	364	chicken vindaloo	580–700
	994	chapati	120

whole pizza   500–800

Sandwiches – using sliced white bread:

fish – one piece deep fried		liver sausage	480
in batter	325	roast beef	390
portion chips	325	cheese and tomato	445
	650	chicken salad	435
		ham	410

3 spare ribs	190
fried rice with pork and	
shrimps	210
egg fu yong	395
sweet-and-sour pork	520
beef chop suey	280
chicken chow mein	260
	1855

CARD GAMES

Andrew Pennycock: The Book of Card Games

For those innocents who think that Bridge is Bridge is Bridge, here are a few of the varieties of the game, along with some variations on Canasta.

Bridge	*Canasta*
Chinese (two-handed)	Bolivian
Chinese (four-handed)	Brazilian
Contract	Chilean
Contract Nullos	Cuban

Bridge	Canasta
Cut-Throat	Cut-Throat
Domino	Five-Handed
Double-Dummy	Hollywood
Draw	Italian
Ecarte	Joker
German	Racehorse
Goulash	Six-Handed
Honeymoon	Three-Handed
Japanese	Three-Pack
Memory	Two-Handed
Passing	Uruguay
Reject	
Reverse	
Single Dummy	
Strip	
Trio	
Turnover	
Widow	

CARS

Most popular colours for Ford's British Range, 1981

The lists below show the top three colours for each Ford model ordered:

MODEL	EXTERIOR	INTERIOR
Escort		
Of the 102 625 sold:	Sunburst Red – 18.7%	Shark Grey – 46.1%
	Caribbean Blue – 11.1%	Blue – 25.8%
	Diamond White – 10.2%	Red – 12.6%
Cortina		
Of the 89 218 sold:	Cardinal Red – 13.5%	Peat – 31.1%
	Sienna Brown – 10.4%	Shark Grey – 29.1%
	Atlantic Blue – 9.9%	Blue – 23.4%

Fiesta
Of the 60 297 sold:

Caribbean Blue – 10.6%	Shark Grey – 36%
Sienna Brown – 10.3%	Blue – 25.7%
Cardinal Red – 9.9%	Red – 18.1%

Granada
Of the 15 193 sold:

Titan Blue – 14.3%	Shark Grey – 33.7%
Crystal Green – 14%	Peat – 24.2%
Champagne Gold – 13.9%	Blue – 21.5%

Capri
Of the 10 094 sold:

Two Tone – 17.3%	Shark Grey – 57.1%
Cardinal Red – 12.1%	Blue – 22.3%
Titan Blue – 9.4%	Tan – 16.9%

Car Ownership –
international comparison, 1978

U.N. International Road Federation

Numbers of cars per 1000 population

USA	530
Luxembourg	425
Australia	381
West Germany	346
Sweden	345
France	327
Belgium	302
Netherlands	294
Italy	286
Denmark	276
United Kingdom	262
Irish Republic	194
Japan	184
Yugoslavia	85
Greece	80
Brazil	66
Chile	31

The above figures include both private and company-owned cars.

Difficult cars to sell

According to car dealer James Gilgallon, these are the part exchanges most dealers would rather not be offered, thank you very much.

1　Any Alfa except Sud
2　*BL*: Maxi autos, Marina, Princess, XJ12, Daimler 66
3　*Talbot:* Avenger estate, Chrysler 2-litre
4　*Datsun:* SSS Coupe, Laurel, Skyline, 280C
5　*Ford:* Cortina 2.3cc, Granada fuel-injection
6　*Fiat:* 132 2-litre
7　*GM:* Ascona Rekord, Vauxhall Carlton
8　*Lancia:* Betas, Gammas
9　*Colt:* Sigma, Sapporo
10　*Citroen:* Reflex, Athena
11　Any East European marque
12　Vans that stink of fish

CHANCELLORS OF THE EXCHEQUER

Since 1905, only three of our Chancellors have been trained economists – Dalton, Gaitskell and Jenkins. The rest were:

Lawyers	9
Historians	4
Classicists	4
Mathematicians	2
Chemists	2
Accountant	1
Iron Merchant	1
Rag Trader	1

Do you think we would have been better off with more economists at the Exchequer or with fewer? Hmm. We have recently had a trained economist in complete charge, Sir Harold

Wilson, but that didn't do us much good. Mrs Thatcher is a chemist. Is it any good having faith or hope in any of them? Let's move on to charity instead . . .

CHARITIES
Income of UK charities, 1979–80

Charities Aid Foundation

	£ million
National Trust	23.6
Dr Barnardo's	20.6
Salvation Army	19.2
Oxfam	18.8
Imperial Cancer Research Fund	15.2
Spastics' Society	15.1
Cancer Research Campaign	13.7
Royal National Institute for the Blind	11.8
Royal National Lifeboat Institution	10.1
Save the Children	10.0
British Red Cross	8.4
Help the Aged	7.3
Christian Aid	7.2
Royal Society for the Prevention of Cruelty to Children	6.7
Royal British Legion	6.4
Marie Curie Memorial Foundation	4.8

CHAT
Ten worst chat-up lines

As published in *The Standard*'s Ad Lib column – compiled by John Blake with the assistance of Small Sheila and Big Rosie.

1   Cheer up, darling, it might never happen.
2   Do you come here often?

3   If you play your cards right, you can have me tonight.
4   You must be Scorpio/Virgo/Cancer, etc.
5   Do you believe in love at first sight?
6   Normally, I wouldn't dream of doing this . . .
7   Has anyone ever told you that you have beautiful eyes?
8   You're not one of those women's libbers, are you?
9   Haven't I seen you somewhere before?
10 You know, you look just like Jane Fonda/Meryl Streep/
     Lady Di/Barbara Woodhouse, etc.

CHUNNELS

In January 1982, there were eight fat dossiers sitting on the desk of the head of the Ministry of Transport's Channel Tunnel Unit in London. Five were in favour of a tunnel, two in favour of bridge *and* tunnel, one in favour of a bridge. One of these centuries, a decision will finally be made. Could it be by 1983?

1   British and French railways propose a single track, bored tunnel, six metres in diameter. Cost £800m, plus £250m for works on land.
2   European Channel Tunnel Group (an international consortium advised by Rothschilds) offers several schemes including a cut-price tunnel costing £539m.
3   Cross-channel Contractors (a British consortium of Taylor Woodrow, Balfour Beatty and Edmund Nuttall, advised by Morgan Grenfell) propose a six- or seven-metre tunnel.
4   Tarmac (advised by Robert Fleming) propose twin seven-metre tunnels large enough for trains carrying cars or lorries, built in three stages: £900m for the first tunnel, £450m for road/rail terminals and £500m for the second tunnel. Wimpey (advised by Kleinwort Benson) agreed with Tarmac and joined them.
5   John Laing propose to prefabricate tunnel sections and sink them together on the seabed. Cost unknown.

6   Linkintoeurope proposes a suspension bridge carrying a six-lane motorway costing £1 750m.
7   Eurobridge Studies (advised by Morgan Grenfell) would like to build a 12-lane motorway, with a rail tunnel. Total cost £3 245m.
8. British Steel (advised by Lazards) envisage a combination of two road viaducts and a road/rail tunnel costing £3 800m.

CHURCHES
Church attendance in England

Bible Society: Prospects for the 80s

	thousands		percentage change
	1975	1979	1975–1979
Protestant churches			
Episcopal	1 302	1 256	−3.5
Methodist	454	447	−1.5
Baptist	193	203	+5.2
United Reformed and Congregational	150	139	−7.3
Independant	167	206	+23.4
African and West Indian	55	66	+20.0
Pentecostal and Holiness	78	88	+12.8
Other	122	128	+4.9
All Protestant churches	2 521	2 533	+0.5
Roman Catholic	1 418	1 310	−7.6
Orthodox	6	7	+16.7
All churches	3 945	3 850	−2.4

In 1979, 18% of the adult population of England belonged to a Christian church. Regional variations are considerable – Merseyside 35%; Lancashire 32%; Humberside 11%.

Only 11% of the total population actually *attend* church regularly.

CITIES
Top Ten Cities

Census 1981, Preliminary Report for Towns

	population on census night April 5, 1981	last census place
Greater London	6 696 008	1
Birmingham	920 389	2
Liverpool	510 306	3
Sheffield	477 142	5
Manchester	449 168	4
Leeds	448 528	6
Bristol	387 977	7
Coventry	314 124	8
Bradford	280 691	10
Leicester	279 791	13

Bad news for Manchester. According to the latest census reports, Sheffield has overtaken Manchester in the Big City league. Manchester is now only the fifth biggest English city. There could be even worse blows to Mancunian pride in the next few years. Look at Leeds. What an upstart. It's now just a few hundred people smaller than Manchester.

The population of all ten of the largest English cities have fallen and there is now no centre outside London with more than a million. Birmingham's has dropped from 1 110 000 to 920 000 in the past 20 years, but it remains by far the largest English city other than London.

Third place is held by Liverpool, whose population has fallen by almost half to 510 000 in the past 20 years.

Most expensive cities in the world, 1981

Business International

Tokyo	160.4
Lagos	152.1
Buenos Aires	146.5
London	133.6
Oslo	128.9

Abidjan	128
Stockholm	127.8
Helsinki	123.6
Vienna	120.2
Zurich	120.1

Tokyo is the world's most expensive city, with London the dearest in Europe and the Scandinavian capitals not far behind. Taking New York as the base city with a cost of living index of 100, the Japanese capital had an index of 160.4, displacing Lagos (152.1). The cheapest listed – Lima, Peru – had an index of 77.1.

Over half the cities surveyed had inflation rates of over 15 per cent and some, like Lima, Tel Aviv and Buenos Aires, were close to 100 per cent.

COMICS

Many of the comics below are no longer with us but they will always be fondly remembered. How many can you remember? How many are you still reading?

Adventure	Film Fun
Battle Action	Funnies
Beano	Girl
Beezer	Girl's Crystal
Boy's Fun	Happy Days
Bunty	Hotspur
Buster	Jack and Jill
Butterfly	Jackpot
Champion	Jester
Chips	Jingles
Comet	Judy
Comic Cuts	Knockout
Comicolour	Larks
Cor!	Magic
Cute Fun	Merry and Bright
Dandy	Nutty
Eagle	Playbox

Playhour
Radio Fun
Rainbow
Robin
Rover
Roy of the Rovers
School Friend
Scramble
Shiver and Shake
Slick Fun
Sun

Swift
Tiger
Tiger Tim's Weekly
Tip-Top
Topper
TV Fun
2000 AD
Valour
Victor
Whizzer & Chips
Whoopee

CONTRACEPTION

DHSS

Below are the methods of contraception chosen or recommended by family planning clinics to their clients (as a percentage of all those counselled – a total of 1.6 million clients).

	1975*	1980**
Oral contraceptives	69	54
IUD	14	21
Cap/diaphragm	6	8
Sheath	6	10
Chemicals	1	1
Other	2	2
None	3	5

*Great Britain
**England and Wales only

CORGIS

Royal Corgis, of course. None of your rubbish. Here are their names so look out for them next time you're at a Royal Garden Party at Buckingham Palace.

The Royal Corgis

Brush	Jolly	Chipper
Shadow	Myth	Piper
Sparky	Fable	
Smoky	Socks	

CREEPS

In 1982, two newspapers asked their readers to name their 'Creep of the Year'. This game was a great favourite with readers of both *The New Musical Express* and the Ad Lib pages of *The Standard*. A careful analysis of their results produced the following list.

The Ultimate Creeps of 1982

1   Adam Ant (top of both polls)
2   Margaret Thatcher (second in both)
3   Julio Iglesias
4   Ronald Reagan (only a whisker behind Señor Iglesias)
5   Tony Benn
6   Ken Livingstone (exclusively the choice of *Standard* readers)
7   Errol (a *NME* columnist)
8   Steve Strange
9   Michael Foot
10 {Ian Paisley
     {Paul Morley (another *NME* man – the readers there really loathe their writers)

CRICKET
Sixes I

The vulgar and ungentlemanly practice of hitting balls over the boundary for six seems to evoke a peculiar satisfaction among the paying customers. The following batsmen so forgot themselves as to destroy the peace of the English summer by repeating the feat off several successive balls.

Sixes off six successive balls

G. St. A. Sobers	off M. A. Nash	Notts v Glamorgan	Swansea	1968

Sixes off five successive balls

A. W. Wellard	off T. R. Armstrong	Somerset v Derbys	Wells	1936
A. W. Wellard	off F. E. Woolley	Somerset v Kent	Wells	1938
D. W. Lindsay	off W. T. Greensmith	S. A. Fezela XI v Essex	Chelmsford	1961

Sixes off four successive balls

R. E. Foster	off W. G. Grace	Oxford U. v London Co.	Oxford	1900
E. R. T. Holmes	off J. C. Masterman and J. P. F. Campbell	Oxford U. v Free Foresters	Oxford	1927
J. H. Parsons	off O. C. Scott	Warwicks v West Indies	Birmingham	1928
A. Jepson	off J. H. Wardle	Notts v Yorks	Bradford	1952
R. Benaud	off R. Tattersall	Australia v T. N. Pearce's XI	Scarborough	1953
D. W. White	off J. D. Piachaud	Hants v Oxford U.	Oxford	1960
C. C. Inman	off N. W. Hill	Leics v Notts	Nottingham	1965
Majid Khan	off R. C. Davis	Pakistan v Glamorgan	Swansea	1967
A. W. Greig	off P. J. Lewington	Sussex v Warwicks	Hastings	1975
C. E. B. Rice	off K. W. R. Fletcher	Notts v Essex	Nottingham	1976
F. C. Hayes	off M. A. Nash	Lancs v Glamorgan	Swansea	1977
M. A. Nash	off D. Breakwell	Glamorgan v Somerset	Taunton	1978
M. J. Procter	off D. Breakwell	Glos v Somerset	Taunton	1979

Procter actually hit six successive balls from Breakwell for six, four off the end of one over and two from the first two balls of his next one.

And hats off to Malcolm Nash who, having twice appeared in this list as a victim bowler, turned the tables in 1978 at Taunton to join the batsmen.

Sixes II

Six-hitters tend not to stop at a single match. Lancashire's bowlers at Blackpool in 1959, when Warwickshire's Jim Stewart hit 17 sixes in the game, must have wished that they never started.

Five players have exceeded 45 sixes in an English season:

number of sixes in season	player	county	year
72	Arthur Wellard	Somerset	1935
57	Arthur Wellard	Somerset	1936
57	Arthur Wellard	Somerset	1938
51	Arthur Wellard	Somerset	1933
49	John Edrich	Surrey	1965
48	Arthur Carr	Notts	1925
46	Fred Barrett	Notts	1928
46	Hugh Bartlett	Sussex	1938

Bowlers' Nightmares

The weather and the state of our pitches have not traditionally made for huge run-scoring in England, but 1450 runs in a match has been achieved fourteen times – half of them, not surprisingly, in test matches not restricted to the traditional three days.

1723 for 31 wickets	England v Australia	Leeds	1948
1601 – 29	England v Australia	Lord's	1930
1507 – 28	England v West Indies	Oval	1976
1502 – 28	MCC v New Zealanders	Lord's	1927
1499 – 31	T. N. Pearce's XI v Australians	Scarborough	1961
1496 – 24	England v Australia	Nottingham	1938
1494 – 37	England v Australia	Oval	1934
1492 – 33	Worcs v Oxford U.	Worcester	1904
1477 – 32	Hants v Oxford U.	Southampton	1913
1477 – 33	England v South Africa	Oval	1947
1475 – 27	Northants v Surrey	Northampton	1920
1469 – 30	Surrey v Cambridge U.	Oval	1921
1458 – 31	England v South Africa	Nottingham	1947
1451 – 36	Sussex v Kent	Hastings	1929

These scores are put in a somewhat less awe-inspiring perspective in that while just four match aggregates of 1500 and more have been recorded in England, 69 such unseemly totals have been recorded abroad.

The accumulators

The reward for hours of patience at the crease. The following batsmen have scored more than 40000 runs in their playing careers:

Jack Hobbs	Surrey, between 1905 and 1934	61 237
Frank Woolley	Kent, 1906–38	58 959
'Patsy' Hendren	Middx, 1907–38	57 611
Philip Mead	Hants, 1905–36	55 061
W. G. Grace	Glos, London County, 1865–1908	54 211
Walter Hammond	Glos, 1920–51	50 551
Herbert Sutcliffe	Yorks, 1919–45	50 138
Tom Graveney	Glos, Worcs, 1948–71	47 793
Tom Hayward	Surrey, 1893–1914	43 551
Colin Cowdrey	Oxford U., Kent, 1950–76	42 719
Andrew Sandham	Surrey, 1911–37	41 284
Geoffrey Boycott	Yorks, 1962–	40 152
Leonard Hutton	Yorks, 1934–60	40 140

All of them, of course, scored a significant proportion of their runs in test matches for England.

Famous English test cricketers not born in England

	birthplace	debut
R. O. Butcher	St Philip (Barbados)	1981
M. C. Cowdrey	Bangalore (India)	1954
B. L. D'Oliveira	Cape Town (South Africa)	1966
M. H. Denness	Bellside (Scotland)	1969
P. H. Edmonds	Lusaka (Zambia)	1975

A. W. Grieg	Queenstown (South Africa)	1972
A. R. Lewis	Swansea (Wales)	1969
R. A. Woolmer	Kanpur (India)	1975

CROSSWORD CLUES

Edmund Akenhead has been the editor of *The Times* crossword, the greatest of them all, for many years. Here are three of his favourite clues:

1   (Set by Adrian Bell, who composed the first ever *Times* crossword)
    The cylinder's jammed (5, 4)
    Answer: Swiss roll
2   (Set by Akenhead while working for newspapers in East Africa)
    Cinderella's midnight music (7)
    Answer: Ragtime
3   (Set for a *Times* competition crossword)
    They hang from trees in the book of Jeremiah (6)
    Answer: Amenta*

*The solution, incidentally, is that 'amenta' is not only the plural of 'amentum', or catkin, but also hidden in the word 'lamentations', as in *The Lamentations of Jeremiah*.

DARTS
Pick of the pubs

The oldest national darts team championship in the world was established in 1938 by *The People* newspaper; since 1962 it has been run by the National Darts Association. Here are the winners since the NDA took over:

1963–64	Brown Bear, Hanworth, Middlesex
1964–66	(no contest)
1966–67	Brown Bear, Hanworth, Middlesex
1967–68	Conquering Hero, Wigan, Lancashire

1968–69	Glyn Neath Social Club, Glyn Neath, Glamorgan
1969–70	White Lion Hotel, Oakham, Rutland
1970–71	Elephant Hotel, Pontefract, Yorkshire
1971–72	Priory Social Club, Middlesbrough, Yorkshire
1972–73	Bird in Hand, Ironbridge, Shropshire
1973–74	York Hotel, Bolton, Lancashire
1974–75	Courage Social Club, Reading, Berkshire
1975–76	Forresters Arms, Shepshed, Leicestershire
1976–77	Charcoal Burner, Crawley, Sussex
1977–78	Eyres Monsell Club, Leicester
1978–79	(no contest)
1979–80	Conservative Club, Ipswich, Suffolk
1980–81	Alhambra Bar, Bellshill, Strathclyde

The language of darts

Someone listening to a darts commentary for the first time could be forgiven for being utterly confused. By the strange intonation – and by the words. Here are a few of them:

Bed – narrow bands marked by wiring: double, treble, 25
Bull – centre of board
Check-out – means of finishing a game
Leg – game
Maximum – 180 score
Oche – raised marker, wood or metal, which indicates the minimum throwing distance
Outer bull – 25 band (outer centre ring)
Pull – the player pulls a dart when he deliberately throws it just outside the double, to serve as a marker or guide
Red bit – treble 20
Segment – the board is divided into 20 segments, 1–20
Shanghai – the player wins regardless of his opponent's score if he gets a treble, single and double consecutively on any one number on the board. This does not apply to professional darts
Shot-out – Means of finishing a game
Ton – 100 score

DEATH
Odd ends

Fulk Fitzwarine (1230?–1264)   During the retreat from the Battle of Lewes his horse got stuck in a swamp and Fitzwarine was asphyxiated inside his heavy armour.

The Earl of Morton (1525–1581)   Was beheaded by a type of guillotine called a 'maiden' which he himself had introduced while Regent of Scotland.

Francis Bacon (1561–1626)   One wintry day the celebrated philosopher killed a chicken and stuffed its carcass with snow in an experiment to discover whether chilled meat could be preserved. Alas, the severe chill he caught himself in the process failed to preserve him.

Thomas May (1595–1650)   Because he was grossly fat, May used 'slings' made of strips of cloth to support his enormous sagging chins. During one gargantuan meal the slings prevented him swallowing properly and he suffocated.

Thomas Otway (1652–1685)   This poverty-stricken playright resorted to begging in the street. One day he was given a guinea piece and hurried to buy a bread roll. After only a few bites of his first food for days he was seized by a terrible choking fit and died.

Arnold Bennett (1867–1931)   A highly successful novelist, Bennett caught typhoid and died after drinking a glass of water in Paris to demonstrate to his companions that the tap water was perfectly safe.

DISEASE
Notification of selected infectious diseases in the UK

Office of Population Censuses and Surveys

| | *thousands* | | |
	1971	*1976*	*1980*
Tuberculosis			
respiratory	10.8	9.2	7.8
other	3.0	2.6	2.7

Whooping cough	19.4	4.4	22.8
Measles	155.2	68.4	148.0

	numbers		
Diphtheria	17	2	5
Acute poliomyelitis			
paralytic	7	12	2
non-paralytic	3	3	1
Tetanus	24	15	18

For the first time in three years there were notifications of diphtheria in 1980. Notifications of measles were the highest for three years. The incidence of acute poliomyelitis has fallen from over 2500 cases in 1951 to just 3 cases in 1980.

DIVORCE
Reasons for divorce

The following reasons for divorce, all taken from recent records of the London divorce courts, were reported in *The Times*. So they must be true, mustn't they.

George Blake: for treason   1967
Frank Canty: for reading endlessly in the lavatory   1968
Leonard Dedman: for an obsessive love of Chinese food   1970
Michael Nightingale: for endless yawning   1970
Andrew Beazley: for continual whistling   1973
Sally Palmer: for continual giggling   1975
Eugene Jennings: for over-weening ambition   1976
Sheila Lewcock: for limiting lovemaking to once a week   1979
Donald Napier: for making endless puns   1979
Pauline Paul: for not wearing make-up   1980
Michael Rowley: putting cricket before his family   1981

DOMESTIC APPLIANCES
Most commonly owned
DHSS: Social Trends

Percentage of households with:	1970	1979
telephone	35	67
washing machine	65	77
refrigerator	66	92
deep-freeze	—	47
car	52	58
central heating	30	55
colour TV	2	66
black-and-white TV only	90	30

Ownership of consumer durables has increased at a higher rate among the semi-skilled and unskilled manual groups than among other groups.

Estimated service life

	years
electric cooker	12
gas cooker	13
refrigerator	15
freezer	20
washing machine	11
electric drier	14
dishwasher	11
black-and-white TV	11
colour TV	12

That's what the trade would have us believe. Don't bank on it.

DRAMA
The Standard drama awards, 1981

Most promising playwright: Nell Dunn for 'Steaming'
Best play: 'Passion Play' by Peter Nichols
Best musical: 'Cats' by Andrew Lloyd Webber
Best comedy: 'Goose Pimples' by Mike Leigh
The Sidney Edwards Award, for the best director: Sir Peter Hall for 'The Oresteia'
Best actor: Alan Howard in 'Good'
Best actress: Maggie Smith in 'Virginia'
Special award: The Royal Shakespeare Company
Ballet award: Peter Wright, Director at Sadlers Wells Royal Ballet
Opera award: Sir Peter Hall for 'Midsummer Night's Dream' at Glyndebourne

EARNINGS
Workers' earnings
DoE: Earnings Survey

Gross weekly earnings of full-time employees.

	1970 £	1980 £
Central government	30.3	135.1
Local authorities	30.2	125.2
Public corporations	29.1	128.8
All public sector	29.6	128.2
Private sector	29.7	122.2
All employees	29.7	124.5

To be amongst the top 10% of male wage earners in 1980, you had to earn at least £179 per week. Between 1970 and 1980 average earnings of male full-time employees have increased by 315 per cent.

Manual Workers' Pay League, 1981

DoE: Earnings Survey

Weekly gross earnings including basic rates, overtime, premiums and incentive payments. 1976 league placings in brackets.

occupation		1976 £	1981 £
1	Coalface workers (3)	80.7	165.3
2	Print compositors (8)	74.3	164.2
3	Steel erectors (2)	81.6	162.9
4	Print machine minders (21)	70.9	155.2
5	Dockers (1)	83.5	153.8
6	Gas fitters (14)	72.6	150.7
	Electricity workers (7)	74.4	150.7
8	Site electricians (5)	76.0	143.9
9	Print machine assistants (20)	71.1	140.6
10	Maintenance fitters (12)	72.9	140.4
11	Electricians (16)	72.4	138.6
12	Chemical workers (15)	72.6	137.3
13	Seamen (11)	73.5	136.4
14	Cable linesmen (—)	65.4	135.1
	Crane drivers (10)	73.6	135.1
16	Platers/shipwrights (4)	76.2	134.6
17	Skilled welders (9)	74.1	133.9
18	Heating fitters (—)	63.8	133.7
19	Train drivers (6)	74.5	132.9
20	Bus drivers (18)	71.6	131.6
21	Signalmen/shunters (13)	72.8	130.6
22	Ambulancemen (19)	71.3	130.3
23	Lorry drivers (—)	67.5	127.8
24	Electrical fitters (17)	72.0	127.7
	Installation fitters (25)	68.6	127.7

Top people's annual earnings, 1980

Civil Service	£
Head of the Home Civil Service ⎫	
Permanent Secretary to the Treasury ⎬	33 500
Secretary to the Cabinet ⎭	
Permanent Secretary	31 000
Second Permanent Secretary	28 500
Deputy Secretary	24 500
Under Secretary	20 500

Armed Forces	
Admiral of the Fleet ⎫	
Field Marshal ⎬	33 500
Marshal of the Royal Air Force ⎭	
Admiral ⎫	
General ⎬	31 000
Air Chief Marshal ⎭	
Vice Admiral ⎫	
Lieutenant General ⎬	24 500
Air Marshal ⎭	
Medical Rear Admiral ⎫	
Medical Major General ⎬	21 500
Medical Air Vice Marshal ⎭	
Rear Admiral ⎫	
Major General ⎬	20 500
Air Vice-Marshal ⎭	

Judiciary	
Lord Chief Justice	40 000
Master of the Rolls ⎫	
Lord of Appeal ⎬	37 000
Lord President of the Court of Session ⎭	
Lord Chief Justice (Scotland/Northern Ireland) ⎫	35 500
President of the Family Division ⎬	
Lord Justice of Appeal (Northern Ireland) ⎫	33 500
Lord Justice Clerk (Scotland) ⎬	

How did they all manage? Luckily, since 1980 their salaries have gone up considerably.

Some assorted earnings, 1980

	£
Paul McCartney	25 million
Lord Grade (when head of ACC)	207 854
Sir Maurice Hodgson, Chairman of ICI	124 380
Ian MacGregor, Chairman of British Steel	48 500
Mrs Thatcher, Prime Minister	31 750
Dr Runcie, Archbishop of Canterbury	12 590

EMPLOYEES IN THE UK, 1980

DES: Social Trends

	thousands
Manufacturing	6 808
Professional & scientific services	3 717
Distributive trades	2 790
Miscellaneous services	2 519
Public administration	1 596
Transport and communication	1 500
Construction	1 265
Insurance, banking and finance	1 258
Agriculture, forestry and fishing	370
Gas, electricity and water	347
Mining and quarrying	344
Total for all industries and services	22 514

Breakdown of manufacturing figures

Engineering and allied industries	3 121
Rest of manufacturing	1 322
Textiles, leather and clothing	813
Food, drink and tobacco	681
Chemicals, coals and petroleum	470
Metal manufacture	401
	6 808

EPITAPHS

The *Sunday Times* magazine in 1981 asked some well-known living people – well known for living as well as for being well known – to choose a suitable epitaph for themselves.

Duchess of Argyll
    All you that grieve or heave a sigh
    Remember, I might return.

Sir Charles Forte
    Born 26 November 1908. Died 26 November 2008.
    He was a loving Great-grandfather, Grandfather,
    Father and Husband.

Clement Freud, MP
    He very seldom insulted people intentionally.

Terry Gilliam
    I came. I saw. I concurred.

Amanda Lear
    To Let.

Prue Leith
    All her life she fed the famous. Now she feeds the worms.

John Mortimer
    The defence rests.

Molly Parkin
    It's cold down here and lonely
    No lover warms my bed
    Why not pop in and join me
    Share living with the dead?

Esther Rantzen
    Consumers complained to her
    Loudly and faint
    Till she died of her final
    Consuming complaint.

Anthony Shaffer
   The butler did it.

Sir Roy Strong
   Dead but he won't lie down.

EXERCISE
Health Education Council

Different exercises and their effectiveness in promoting stamina, suppleness and strength.

	stamina	*suppleness*	*strength*
Badminton	**	***	**
Canoeing	***	**	***
Climbing stairs	***	*	**
Cricket	*	**	*
Cycling (hard)	****	**	***
Ballroom dancing	*	***	*
Disco dancing	***	****	*
Digging	***	**	****
Football	***	***	***
Golf	*	**	*
Gymnastics	**	****	***
Hill walking	***	*	**
Housework	*	**	*
Jogging	****	**	**
Judo	**	****	**
Rowing	****	**	****
Sailing	*	**	**
Squash	***	***	**
Swimming (hard)	****	****	****
Tennis	**	***	**
Walking briskly	**	*	*
Weightlifting	*	*	****
Yoga	*	****	*

  * no real effect   *** very good effect
 ** beneficial effect   **** excellent effect

A doctor writes:
Reading this book rates **** for eye strength and scores *** for finger suppleness.

EXPENDITURE

After expending all that energy, let us now consider what happens when we expend all this money.

UK expenditure on, and energy content of, food obtained for consumption in the home, 1980

Ministry of Agriculture, Fisheries and Food: National Food Survey

type of food	pence per person per week	energy provided (calories per penny)
Meat	230	11
Bread and other cereals	110	41
Milk, cream and cheese	104	21
Vegetables	80	16
Fruit	44	10
Butter, margarine and other fats	33	74
Fish	32	6
Beverages	28	2
Eggs	19	14
Sugar and preserves	16	88
Other foods	24	10

Calories per week 15,617

Further food notes:
Consumption of coffee has more than doubled in the last 20 years whilst tea consumption has dropped by 28%. In the meat category, the most dramatic rise is in uncooked poultry. We eat double the amount of pork we did in 1961 but consumption of beef and lamb has declined. And the British spent £7.20 a head on food each week in 1980.

Consumer expenditure, 1980

CSO: Social Trends

What the average household spends, expressed as a percentage of total consumer expenditure.

Food	17.2
Housing	14.6
Transport and vehicles	13.8
Alcohol	7.5
Clothing and footwear	7.3
Durable household goods	4.9
Fuel and light	4.7
Tobacco	3.6
Other goods, services and miscellaneous	26.4

Expenditure on food has remained roughly the same (increasing by only 8% since 1966), but expenditure on alcohol, other than beer, has increased by 130%.

FILMS
Top UK box office receipts, 1981

Screen International

1 *Superman II* (A) Col-EMI-Warner
2 *For Your Eyes Only* (A) United Artists
3 *Flash Gordon* (A) Col-EMI-Warner
4 *Snow White and the Seven Dwarfs* (U) Disney
5 *Any Which Way You Can* (AA) Col-EMI-Warner
6 *Clash of the Titans* (A) UIP
7 *Private Benjamin* (AA) Col-EMI-Warner
8 *Raiders of the Lost Ark* (A) UIP
9 *The Elephant Man* (AA) Col-EMI-Warner
10 *Tess* (A) Col-EMI-Warner
11 *The Jazz Singer* (A) Col-EMI-Warner
12 *Chariots of Fire* (A) 20th Century Fox
13 *Airplane* (A) UIP

14 *Caligula* (X) GTO
15 *The Blue Lagoon* (AA) Col-EMI-Warner
16 *Excalibur* (AA) Col-EMI-Warner
17 *History of the World Part I* (AA) Col-EMI-Warner
18 *The Cannonball Run* (A) 20th Century Fox
19 *The Postman Always Rings Twice* (X) ITC
20 *Popeye* (U) Disney

Portrait of a declining industry

Department of Trade

Feature films – by type of certificate

	1971	1980
U	98	25
A	77	82
AA	77	84
X	228	124
Certificate refused	22	4
Total films submitted	502	319

Cinemas

Cinema complexes	1 420	978
Admissions	176 millions	111.9 millions
Average admission charge	34 pence	113 pence

The number of films submitted to the British Board of Film Censors fell by 40% between 1974 and 1980.

The ten best Ealing films

George Perry knows a lot about movies – he's been writing articles on the subject for twenty years. He's also written the book *Forever Ealing* so we asked him to pick his top ten from that illustrious British studio:

1 *Kind Hearts and Coronets* (1949)
2 *The Ladykillers* (1955)
3 *Passport to Pimlico* (1949)
4 *Dead of Night* (1945)

5 *Whisky Galore!* (1949)
6 *The Lavender Hill Mob* (1951)
7 *The Man in the White Suit* (1951)
8 *It Always Rains on Sunday* (1947)
9 *Hue and Cry* (1947)
10 *Went the Day Well?* (1943)

The ten best Pinewood films

George Perry also knows a lot about Pinewood Studios (he wrote yet another book, called *Movies from the Mansion*, to prove it). Here are his top ten from there:

1 *Oliver Twist* (1947)
2 *The Browning Version* (1950)
3 *The Red Shoes* (1947)
4 *Pygmalion* (1938)
5 *Dr No* (1962)
6 *Superman II* (1980)
7 *A High Wind in Jamaica* (1964)
8 *Young and Innocent* (1937)
9 *Black Narcissus* (1946)
10 *Genevieve* (1952)

FOOTBALL

Total attendance at Football League matches

Football League/Scottish Football League

| year | thousands | |
	England and Wales	Scotland
1961–62	27 979	3 979
1966–67	28 902	3 242
1971–72	28 700	3 338
1976–77	26 182	3 168
1978–79	24 540	3 114
1979–80	24 003	3 031
1980–81	21 908	2 527

There has been a continuous fall since the Second World War. Television coverage, hooliganism, costs, boring games are some of the reasons usually trotted out. In the 1980–81 season, several clubs experimented by playing fixtures on Sundays. In most cases, these matches attracted a higher crowd than the Saturday average.

The football teams followed by 20 famous people

1	David Hamilton	Fulham
2	Pete Murray	Arsenal
3	Hylda Baker	Bolton Wanderers
4	Eric Morecambe	Luton Town
5	Bernie Winters	Arsenal
6	Peter Cook	Tottenham Hotspur
7	Ted Rogers	Chelsea
8	Lance Percival	Chelsea
9	Eric Morley	Arsenal
10	Jimmy Hill	Coventry City
11	Lorraine Chase	Millwall
12	Jasper Carrott	Birmingham City
13	Elton John	Watford
14	Brian Moore	Gillingham
15	Mike Yarwood	Stockport County
16	Ed Stewart	Everton
17	Tim Brooke-Taylor	Derby County
18	Eddie Large	Manchester City
19	Arthur Mullard	Arsenal
20	Trevor Nunn	Ipswich Town

Long-serving managers

Long-serving managers in the Football League are barely more plentiful than long-serving kamikaze pilots, but a few have managed to survive the fluctuating attitudes of directors, players and crowds for a creditable period of time. The following managers were all still with their respective clubs on 1 March 1982.

manager	club	appointed
Bobby Robson	Ipswich Town	January 1969
Jimmy Frizzell	Oldham Athletic	March 1970
Lawrie McMenemy	Southampton	June 1973
Bob Paisley	Liverpool	July 1974
John Lyall	West Ham United	August 1974
Brian Clough	Nottingham Forest	January 1975
Bobby Roberts	Colchester United	June 1975
David Smith	Southend United	May 1976
Terry Neill	Arsenal	8 July 1976
Keith Burkinshaw	Tottenham Hotspur	14 July 1976

The worst of the worst

A list, by division, of the five clubs with the lowest single home attendance figure in the 1980–81 season. Clubs marked with an asterisk (*) were relegated at the end of the season.

club	opponents	attendance
DIVISION ONE		
Crystal Palace*	Birmingham	9 820
Stoke City	Ipswich	10 722
Middlesbrough	Brighton	11 076
Coventry	Brighton	11 462
Brighton	Middlesbrough	12 112
DIVISION TWO		
Wrexham	Bristol Rovers	3 220
Bristol Rovers*	Notts County	3 552
Cambridge United	Cardiff City	3 790
Orient	Bolton Wanderers	3 824
Cardiff City	Cambridge United	4 059

DIVISION THREE

Colchester United*	Carlisle United	1 430
Chester	Newport County	1 640
Hull City*	Newport County	2 059
Oxford United	Chester	2 526
Millwall	Oxford United	2 781

DIVISION FOUR

Halifax Town	Bournemouth	987
Tranmere Rovers	Scunthorpe United	1 063
York City	Northampton Town	1 167
Bradford City	Hereford United	1 249
Rochdale	Stockport County	1 291

In Scotland, not all clubs give accurate gate figures, and particularly in the lower divisions the attendance figures tend to be estimated approximations.

club	opponents	attendance

SCOTTISH PREMIER DIVISION

Kilmarnock*	Morton	973
Airdrieonians	Morton	1 600
Partick Thistle	Kilmarnock	1 600
Heart of Midlothian*	Kilmarnock	1 866
Rangers	Morton	2 500

SCOTTISH FIRST DIVISION

Dumbarton	Hamilton Acad.	300
Clydebank	Berwick Rangers	350
Stirling Albion*	Hamilton Acad.	350
Berwick Rangers*	Stirling Albion	510
East Stirling	Dumbarton	550

SCOTTISH SECOND DIVISION

Albion Rovers	Three separate opponents	150
Meadowbank Thistle	Five separate opponents	150
Stenhousemuir	Brechin City	150
Cowdenbeath	Stranraer	200
Stranraer	Three separate opponents	200

FREIGHT
Odd air freight

British Airways Cargo reckon that the only animal they have not so far carried is a giraffe, though Malcolm Parr, senior P.R.O., admits they might turn up their noses at a consignment of skunks. Otherwise, pretty well anything has gone by air:

Flyers Flown – Eight baby starlings abandoned in England by their emigrating parents were flown to Kenya and released into summertime there.

Rocket Flies 150 Years Late – A full-size working replica of Stephenson's Rocket weighing 8 tons flew to an exhibition in California.

Jumbo Stork – Calf embryos conceived in Britain were flown to New Zealand inside special cannisters containing liquid nitrogen and then transferred into the bodies of host 'mother' cows which later gave birth to healthy young.

Here Today There Yesterday – Very shortlived radioactive isotopes for use in medical operations have been flown from London to New York by Concorde.

Air Piracy – In 1981 British Airways Cargo carried the most valuable air freight consignment in history when it flew all the treasures for the Japanese Exhibition to London.

Flied Eggs – The eggs of endangered species of birds laid under special conditions in Britain were flown back for hatching in their native environments.

Air Race – Twenty-six Formula I racing cars were airlifted to South Africa for the 1982 Grand Prix. This cargo was worth more than £2½ million.

Flying School – A number of dolphins rescued from slaughter by fishermen in the Far East were taken to new waters by British Airways Cargo.

Winged Speech – In December 1981 British Airways delivered dozens of pre-recordings of the Queen's Christmas Message to places ranging from Mauritius to remote Pacific Islands.

GAMES PEOPLE PLAY, 1980

General Household Survey: Social Trends

Percentage of people in Great Britain participating in sport during the most popular quarter for that pastime.

	men	women
Walking	22	22
Billiards/snooker	14	2
Darts	13	4
Swimming (indoors)	8	9
Outdoor swimming	7	8
Fishing	6	1
Football	6	—
Golf	6	1
Squash	4	2
Table tennis	4	2
Tennis	4	2
Cricket	3	—
Cycling	2	1
Ten-pin bowling/indoor bowls	2	1
Sailing	1	—
Keep fit/yoga	1	4
Gymnastics/indoor athletics	1	—
Horse riding	1	1
Rambling/hiking	1	1

GHOSTS
Some castles and some of their reputed ghosts

Astley – The Duke of Suffolk, father of Lady Jane Grey
Blackness – General Dalyell, founder of the Scots Greys (now Royal Scots Dragoon Guards)
Caerphilly – A spectral woman whose appearance was a sign of sudden death or disaster

Carlisle – A woman. A large dog. (They can't tell the difference in Carlisle.)
Dunraven – A green lady
Dunstanburgh – Earl of Lancaster, executed for treason in 1322
Dunster – A skeleton
Glamis – A monster. A grey lady. A man with a long beard. Mysterious knockings. A woman with a bundle in her arms. A white Lady. Oh, they've got everything at Glamis
Hadleigh – A wraith
Hermitage – Mary, Queen of Scots
Hever – Ann Boleyn
Inverary – A galley in a lake. A phantom. Ravens
Lancaster – Various unknown figures. (Well that's not going to bring the tourists in.)
Lowther – A coach and horses
Ludlow – Marion de la Bruyere
Nottingham – Queen Isabella
Warwick – Sir Fulke Greville. A large dog
Windsor – Queen Elizabeth in the library. George III

GOLF
Aces in the hole

Many golfers, even bad ones, have fluked a hole in one. Average club golfers are likely to do it more than once in their playing years. This random list is taken from the scorecards and the memories of some of Britain's tournament golfers. The holes in one were recorded in club rounds as well as in tournaments:

19 holes in one	Sandy Herd
18	Henry Cotton
16	James Braid
15	Joe Carr

14	Sid Scott
	Harry Bradshaw
	Ken Bousfield
13	Arthur Lees
11	Dai Rees
	Eric Brown
	Bernard Gallagher
10	J. H. Taylor
	Fred Daly
	Guy Wolstenholme

All these pale somewhat against the 41 holes in one claimed by the American Art Wall.

HATES

Ten of the things young people in Britain hate most; compiled by Adrian Love from letters sent to Radio One's B-15 show:

1 People (especially DJs) who fake Scots accents and refer to all Scotsmen as 'Jimmy'.
2 Flavoured crisps (especially prawn cocktail).
3 Hong Kong-made cassette tapes which unwind as you look at them.
4 Gob-stoppers which won't change colour.
5 Flatmates who forget to replace empty loo rolls.
6 Little old ladies who tell you how they are when you ask them.
7 Nylon shirts with string vests underneath.
8 Men with tight curly perms who wear Crimplene flares with brass buckles, polo-neck sweaters, window-pane check Crimplene jackets and plastic platform shoes.
9 Tomato-shaped ketchup dispensers.
10 IDLAWINTB people: 'I don't like anything which I've never tasted before.'

HEIGHTS

The heights of some famous people

Tom Baker	actor	6ft 3ins
Norris McWhirter	writer	5ft 9ins
Chris Serle	presenter	6ft 5ins
Giant Haystacks	wrestler	6ft 11ins
Sheena Easton	singer	4ft 11ins
Mary Queen of Scots		6ft 2ins
Prince Charles		5ft 10ins
David Bellamy	botanist	6ft 1in
Graham Gooch	cricketer	6ft
Kevin Keegan	footballer	5ft 8ins

HERALDRY

At the College of Arms in Victoria Street, Heralds go about their business of sorting out who can put what on their coat of arms. The list of their own names and titles reads like something out of the Domesday Book.

Richmond Herald
Rouge Croix Pursuivant
Windsor Herald
Somerset Herald
Bluemantle Pursuivant
Rouge Dragon Pursuivant
York Herald
Norroy and Ulster King of Arms
Garter King of Arms
Clarenceux King of Arms

HEROES AND HEROINES
British people's favourite people, 1981

According to a poll conducted among the visitors to Madame Tussaud's in London. (The 1980 placings are in brackets.)

POLITICS
1 Margaret Thatcher   (Margaret Thatcher)
2 { Michael Foot   (Winston Churchill)
    Anwar Sadat   (Michael Foot)
4 { Winston Churchill   (Sir Harold Wilson)
    Shirley Williams   (J. F. Kennedy)

SPORT
1 Bjorn Borg   (Bjorn Borg)
2 John McEnroe   (Kevin Keegan)
3 Sebastian Coe   (Muhammad Ali)
4 { Muhammad Ali   (Johan Cruyff)
    Kevin Keegan   (Geoffrey Boycott)

ENTERTAINMENT
1 Elvis Presley   (Bruce Forsyth)
2 Cliff Richard   (Cliff Richard)
3 Dave Allen   (Liza Minnelli)
4 Liza Minnelli   (The Beatles)
5 Bruce Forsyth   (Elvis Presley)

ARTS
1 Picasso   (Picasso)
2 Leonardo da Vinci   (Beethoven)
    { Salvador Dali   (Rembrandt)
3 { Rudolf Nureyev   (Shakespeare)
    { Shakespeare   (van Gogh)

BEAUTY
1 Princess of Wales   (Sophia Loren)
2 Bo Derek   (Marilyn Monroe)
3 Marilyn Monroe   (Debbie Harry)
4 Sophia Loren   (Brigitte Bardot)
5 Twiggy   (Bo Derek)

HERO OR HEROINE OF ALL TIME

1	Superman	(Superman)
2	Winston Churchill	(Winston Churchill)
3	Joan of Arc	(Martin Luther King)
4	⎧ Clint Eastwood	(Lord Mountbatten)
	⎨ Anwar Sadat	(John Lennon)

FAVOURITE HERO OR HEROINE IN MADAME TUSSAUD'S

1	Princess of Wales	(Tom Baker as Dr Who)
2	Tom Baker as Dr Who	(Lord Carrington)
3	John McEnroe	(Liza Minnelli)
4	Larry Hagman as J.R.	(Elvis Presley)
5	Michael Foot	(Larry Hagman as J.R.)

People most hated and feared

1	Hitler	(Hitler)
2	Ronald Reagan	(Margaret Thatcher)
3	The Yorkshire Ripper	(Idi Amin)
4	Margaret Thatcher	(Ayatollah Khomeini)
5	Leonid Brezhnev	(The Yorkshire Ripper)

Elvis Presley soared from fifth place to 1980 to first place in 'Entertainment' and the Princess of Wales has gone straight to the top of 'Beauty' in her wedding year, overshadowing a bevy of lovely ladies. Bruce Forsyth did not do at all well, plummeting from top to bottom in 'Entertainment'. In Madame Tussaud's Amsterdam poll, Lech Walesa was Number 1 in 'Hero or Heroine of all time'. In London, he didn't make the listings at all.

Meanwhile, the rather younger readers of the *New Musical Express* were generous enough to give their approval to a selection of heroes and fine dressers. The characters they chose might not be the stuff of more conventional heroism, but they make interesting reading none the less. Mr Foot as a fine dresser must be a joke – or was it?

The most wonderful human being

1 Paul Weller (the lead singer of The Jam)
2 David Bowie
3 John Peel
4 Tony Benn
5 Ken Livingstone
6 Clare Grogan (the beautiful singer for the Scottish group, Altered Images)
7 Lech Walesa
8 Mark E. Smith (another singer, this time with The Fall)
9 Princess Diana
10 Kevin Turvey (the alter-ego of comedian Rick Mayall)

The best-dressed person

1 Michael Foot
2 Paul Weller
3 David Sylvian (singer for the group Japan)
4 Adam Ant
5 David Bowie
6 Siouxie Sioux (singer with The Banshees)
7 Toyah Willcox
8 Mark E. Smith
9 Bruce Foxton (another member of The Jam)
10 Princess Diana

HIGHWAY PERSONS

Let's not be sexist. We do have *one* lady highwayman, sorry highwayperson, on our list.

Everybody's heard of Dick Turpin, but he was by no means alone in his toll-gathering activities. Here is David Ashford's list of some of Turpin's less famous colleagues, in no particular order.

Robert King
Captain James Hind
John Cottington – known as 'Mulled Sack'
Captain Richard Dudley
William Davies – known as 'The Golden Farmer'
William Nevison – known as 'Swift Nicks'
Thomas Simpson – known as 'Old Mob'
James Maclaine – known as 'The Gentleman Highwayman'
Claude Duval
John Clavell
Jerry Abershaw
Moll Cutpurse – the only Highwaylady
Captain Philip Stafford
Jack Rann – known as 'Sixteen-String Jack'
Robert Ferguson – known as 'Galloping Dick'
Nicholas Horner
William Page
Jack Bird
Captain James Whitney

HISTORIC SIGHTS

British Tourist Authority

Historic buildings which attracted more than 200,000 paying visitors in 1980:

Windsor Castle Precincts	2 600 000
Tower of London	2 514 900
Edinburgh Castle	919 100
Roman Baths, Bath	679 900
Stonehenge, Wiltshire	618 000
Hampton Court Palace	567 000
Beaulieu, Hampshire	563 400
Wollaton Hall, Nottingham	535 600
Shakespeare's Birthplace, Stratford upon Avon	489 700
Warwick Castle	464 300
Blenheim Palace, Woodstock	354 000

Anne Hathaway's Cottage, Shottery	368 500
Stirling Castle	364 400
Caernarfon Castle	360 400
Palace of Holyroodhouse, Edinburgh	325 800
Broadlands, Hampshire	314 900
Royal Pavilion, Brighton	314 200
Conwy Castle	264 900
Harewood House, West Yorkshire	250 700
Sewerby Hall, Bridlington	250 000
Fountains Abbey, Ripon	234 200
Osborne House, Isle of Wight	228 800
Arundel Castle, West Sussex	225 400
Brontë Parsonage, Haworth	204 500

HOBBIES

Pam Ayres	mountaineering
David Bellamy	ballet
Ronnie Barker	collecting Victoriana
Michael Bentine	Egyptology
Sir Winston Churchill	brick-laying
Deryck Guyler	collecting toy soldiers
Anita Harris	ice skating
Miriam Karlin	interior decorating
Joanna Lumley	junk collecting
Michael Palin	acupuncture
William Rushton	ping-pong
Donald Sinden	ecclesiology
Jim Prior	stamp collecting

HOLIDAYS
Holiday visitors to Britain, 1980

International Passenger Survey, Dept. of Industry

area of residence of visitors	thousands
USA	806
West Germany	692

France	660
Netherlands	440
Ireland	343
Belgium/Luxembourg	307
Middle East	249
Scandinavia	229
Australia	208
Latin America	166
Switzerland	151
Italy	148
Canada	130
Spain	127
Commonwealth Africa	117
Denmark	110
Commonwealth Asia	88
Japan	83
South Africa	76
North Africa	57

Since the peak of 6 million in the Jubilee year of 1977 overseas visitors have dropped in number to 5½ million. We are receiving more visitors from West Germany and the Middle East but less from the USA, Canada, Scandinavia and the Netherlands since 1976.

Holidays abroad –
where we went for our hols

British Tourist Authority

The definition of a holiday is four or more nights spent away from home for non-business purposes.

	percentage of adult Britons visiting	
destination of holiday abroad	1971	1980
Spain	34	23
France	10	16
Italy	8	8
Austria	7	4

West Germany	6	4
Irish Republic	6	4
Switzerland	4	2
Greece	3	7
Netherlands	3	2
Belgium/Luxembourg	3	2
Eastern Europe	1	1
USA	2	7
Other countries	7	7

12 million holidays were taken abroad in 1980 compared with 10¼ million in 1979. The percentage of holidays taken in the USA has more than doubled since 1976. The number of holidays taken in Great Britain is more than three times as many as the number taken abroad – 37 million in 1980 compared with 12 million holidays abroad.

Holiday checklist

It would, of course, be inconceivable for a fashion editor such as Kathy Phillips to go on holiday with just a toothbrush and a pair of flip-flops. This is what she takes (apart from clothing):

Cheque book
Banker's card
Amex
Second wallet
Iron
Adaptors
Hair dryer
Hair grips
Elastic bands
Headband/towelling hat
Brush
Comb (heavy one)
Shampoo
Conditioner and Daniel's gel
Scarves

Rescue Remedy
Elastoplast
Germolene and Calendula
Vitamins (small boxes)
Emery boards
Cotton wool balls
Cotton buds
Tissues
Cleanser
Moisturizer
Beach bag
Scent
Make-up
Laundry bag
Sunglasses

Safety pins	Nail varnish and remover
Scissors	Sun-tan lotion/block/milk
Needles and cotton	Beach towels
Tweezers	Teabags and Hobbs special tea
Aspirin	Books
Alka Seltzer	Writing paper/pens
Kaolin and Morphine	Jewellery box

HOMOSEXUALS

20 famous homosexuals and lesbians

1	Sir Terence Rattigan	playwright
2	Gertrude Stein	writer
3	Guy Burgess	spy
4	Richard the Lionheart	king
5	Graham Chapman	comedian
6	Tom Robinson	singer
7	Quentin Crisp	writer
8	Richard II	king
9	Francis Bacon	philosopher
10	Christopher Marlowe	playwright
11	Lord Byron	poet
12	Oscar Wilde	poet
13	E. M. Forster	writer
14	T. E. Lawrence	soldier-author
15	Christopher Isherwood	playwright
16	Brendan Behan	playwright
17	David Bowie	singer
18	Elton John	singer
19	Gilbert Harding	journalist
20	Virginia Woolf	novelist

HOROSCOPES

We all know a little about the signs of the zodiac and even the least superstitious amongst us takes the occasional look at his or her stars in the morning papers. Less well-known is the Chinese horoscope, which operates by years rather than months. There are eight different signs, which come round every decade in cycles. At the time of publication, in 1982, we are in the middle of the Year of the Dog; for the rest of the decade, the years proceed as follows:

13 February 1983–1 February 1984: Year of the Pig
2 February 1984–19 February 1985: Year of the Rat
20 February 1985–8 February 1986: Year of the Bull
9 February 1986–28 January 1987: Year of the Tiger
29 January 1987–16 February 1988: Year of the Rabbit
17 February 1988–5 February 1989: Year of the Dragon
6 February 1989–26 January 1990: Year of the Snake

Each animal donates a set of characteristics to the humans born under its sign:

Dogs are champions of truth and justice, quite apart from being as devoted, generous, loyal and helpful as you might expect. Although often successful and well-to-do, dogs are the worriers of the Chinese horoscope and often need a bit of encouragement to set them back on their way. Amongst these insecure, but delightful creatures born under the sign of the Dog you will find Charlotte Rampling, Denis Norden, Winston Churchill and a pack of famous foreign dogs from Socrates, to Rasputin to Sophia Loren.

Pigs are lovable, extremely loyal, kind and generous, unashamedly sensual and apt to be naive and defenceless. Famous British Pigs include Elton John, Barbara Cartland, Alfred Hitchcock and Oliver Cromwell.

Rats: the hard-working, intelligent, charming, but acquisitive rat is often underestimated by the other animals as he strives for success. He does, however, have a lighthearted, even frivolous, side to his character. Tell that to Enoch Powell, footballer Billy Wright, Daniel Defoe and William Shakespeare. Foreign rats have included Tolstoy, Mozart, Rubens and Marlon Brando.

Bulls, as you might expect, are the strong, hard-working authority-figures of life, but warm-hearted with it. Mrs Bull is a homebody, but tends to rule the roost – or should it be cowshed? For some reason, bulls tend to be not only politicians, but also showbiz personalities, so the list of British Bulls includes not only Margaret Thatcher, but also Richard Burton, Charlie Chaplin, Twiggy, Shirley Bassey and Benjamin Britten. The same principle applies abroad, amongst Bulls such as Hitler, Napoleon, Nehru, Warren Beatty, Robert Redford and Marlene Dietrich.

Tigers tend to be rebels, leaders of others, charismatic, exciting, but possibly dangerous to know. Well-known tigers amongst us placid British include Isadora Duncan, Val Doonican and Sir Stanley Matthews. Karl Marx, the Ayatollah Khomeini, Evel Kneivel, Beethoven and Marilyn Monroe are, or were, all foreign examples of the breed.

Rabbits are the happiest inhabitants of the Chinese zodiac, being gregarious, sensitive, tender, caring, industrious, determined and successful. They sound appalling, but who could object to Bob Hope (born a British Rabbit), Jimmy Tarbuck, Queen Victoria or Sir Thomas Beecham? Or even Einstein, Confucius, Orson Welles and Frank Sinatra?

Dragons are strong, healthy, fortunate and capable of achieving anything they set their heart on. They love show and display, are talkative and apt to be indiscreet. Flirtatious and convinced of their own superiority they often rush in where even fools would fear to tread – and somehow they survive unscathed. All of this is in vain, however; deep down the dragon feels sad and discontented. Shed a tear of sympathy for Sir Harold Wilson, Edward Heath, Charles Darwin, George Bernard Shaw, John Lennon, Ringo Starr, and such world-shapers as Abraham Lincoln, Freud, Nietzche and Mickey Mouse.

Finally, **Snakes:** these creatures are wise, well-bred, elegant and humorous. They think deeply and are prone to self-criticism. Snakes are kind, loyal friends, but watch out; snakes react sharply to provocation and are very bad losers. So don't cross Julie Christie, Muriel Spark, or Chairman Mao, Picasso, Sartre, Gandhi, John Kennedy or his widow, Jacqueline Kennedy Onassis.

HORSE RACING

Punters' dreams I

The ten longest-priced winners of the Derby, the world's greatest flat race, since the war:

price	horse	jockey	year
66–1	Psidium	Roger Poincelet	1961
50–1	Airborne	Tom Lowrey	1946
50–1	Snow Knight	Brian Taylor	1974
40–1	Pearl Diver	George Brigland	1947
33–1	Never Say Die	Lester Piggott	1954
28–1	Arctic Prince	Charles Spares	1951
25–1	Morston	Edward Hide	1973
22–1	Larkspur	Neville Sellwood	1962
18–1	Hard Ridden	Charlie Smirke	1958
100–8	Phil Drake	Fred Palmer	1955

Punters' dreams II

Everyone has a bet on the Grand National, but outsiders have made us look foolish more often than we care to remember. The bookies are most likely to remember their good fortune in the years the following horses won over the Aintree fences – the eleven longest-priced winners of the Grand National since the war:

price	horse	jockey	year
100–1	Caughoo	Edward Dempsey	1947
100–1	Foinavon	John Buckingham	1967
66–1	Russian Hero	Liam McMorrow	1949
66–1	Ayala	Pat Buckley	1963
50–1	Sheila's Cottage	Arthur Thompson	1948
50–1	Anglo	Tim Norman	1966
40–1	Nickel Coin	Johnny Bullock	1951
40–1	Ben Nevis	Charlie Fenwick	1980
28–1	Nicolaus Silver	Bobby Beasley	1961
28–1	Kilmore	Fred Winter	1962
28–1	Specify	John Cook	1971

Viewed in tandem with Punters' Dreams I, it puts 1947 as the best year for the lucky punter – a judicious £1 win double on Caughoo and Pearl Diver that year would have returned a handy £4040 0s 0d – and there was no betting tax in those days, either.

HOUSES

In 1980, 318,000 people bought property for the first time with the help of a building society mortgage. This is what the average buyer was like.

Nationwide Building Society's stereotype first-time buyer

1 Married couple
2 Early twenties
3 No children
4 Buying older terraced house
5 Not far from the centre of town or city
6 50% secondary income, usually wife's, average £71 per week
7 Primary income £122 per week
8 65% earned less than the national average (£136.70 per week)

9 25% earned less than £100 per week
10 Mortgage repayment over 20–25 years
11 More than 50% paid a deposit of less than £2500
12 Mortgage advance: 77% of purchase price

House prices I:
monthly index average of
second-hand houses

The Times/Halifax index

		index	average price (£)	% change over the preceding year
1977	December	100.0	14 757	
1978	December	121.1	17 868	21.2
1979	December	151.0	22 291	24.8
1980	December	166.2	24 523	10.0
1981	January	167.7	24 752	8.9
1981	February	172.6	25 472	10.5
1981	March	172.9	25 511	9.3
1981	April	170.5	25 164	7.5
1981	May	171.5	25 304	6.0
1981	June	169.5	25 003	3.3
1981	July	167.9	24 779	2.5
1981	August	165.5	24 424	0.9
1981	September	163.1	24 064	−1.7
1981	October	159.7	23 562	−4.1
1981	November	159.0	23 553	−3.9
1981	December	164.1	24 217	−1.3

House prices in *The Times*/Halifax index fell by 1.5% for new homes and 1.3% for second-hand properties during 1981 although the steady downward trend was reversed during December. Regions reflecting the largest falls were Wales, West Midlands and Yorkshire and Humberside.

House prices II: average regional prices of second-hand houses, 1981

	average price (£)	% change over the preceding year
North	18 130	−3.4
York/Humberside	17 494	−2.8
North-west	20 229	1.0
East Midlands	20 360	3.4
West Midlands	21 829	−2.5
East Anglia	23 861	1.7
Wales	18 953	−8.0
South-west	26 696	1.7
South-east	32 425	−0.5
Greater London	32 556	−0.3
Northern Ireland	20 390	6.8
Scotland	22 584	3.1

INTROS

Beginning anything is hard; beginning a novel is not only hard but helps sell novels. Here are five classics selected by the readers of Godfrey Smith's *Sunday Times* column:

1 'It was the afternoon of my eighty-first birthday, and I was in bed with my catamite when Ali announced that the archbishop had come to see me.'
    —Anthony Burgess: *Earthly Powers* (1980)
2 'It is a truth universally acknowledged, that a single man in possession of a good fortune, must be in want of a wife.'
    —Jane Austen: *Pride and Prejudice* (1813)
3 'I wish either my father or my mother, or indeed both of them, as they were both in duty equally bound to it, had minded what they were about when they had begot me;'
    —Laurence Stern: *The Life and Opinions of Tristram Shandy – Gentleman* (1760)

4 'The past is a foreign country; they do things differently there.'
   —L. P. Hartley: *The Go-Between* (1953)
5 'I was set down from the carrier's cart at the age of three; and there with a sense of bewilderment and terror my life in the village began.'
   —Laurie Lee: *Cider with Rosie* (1959)

JOBS
Former jobs of some famous people

1	Jeremy Beadle	writer	taxi driver, DJ, festival promoter, tourist guide, skin-diving instructor, languages teacher
2	Sean Connery	actor	cement mixer, steel bender, coffin polisher
3	Tommy Boyd	presenter	dolphin trainer
4	Des O'Connor	comedian	complaints clerk in a shoe factory
5	Rowan Atkinson	comedian	electrical engineer
6	Cyril Fletcher	comedian	insurance clerk
7	Benny Hill	comedian	weighbridge operator, army driver
8	John Inman	actor	window dresser
9	Cleo Laine	singer	hairdresser's apprentice, pawnbroker's valuer
10	Arthur Mullard	actor	butcher's boy, pro boxer, dance hall bouncer, rag and bone merchant
11	Kate O'Mara	actress	speech therapist
12	Donald Pleasence	actor	railway clerk
13	Jimmy Savile	DJ	miner
14	Harry Secombe	actor	clerk in a mine
15	Bob Todd	actor	cattle breeder
16	Timothy West	actor	furniture salesman
17	Edward Woodward	actor	sanitary engineer
18	David Bellamy	botanist	drain inspector, deckchair attendant

Job availability

General Household Survey, 1980

Source from which those employees lucky enough to get work first heard about the job.

	males %	females %
Employment office/job centre	18	19
Relatives and friends	35	27
Advertisement	21	25
Direct approach to employer	16	16
Private employment agency	3	9
Others (includes careers teachers, professional association, forces resettlement)	6	3

KINGS AND QUEENS

The longest reign was that of Queen Victoria (1837–1901) – 63 years, 216 days. The longest in the world was that of Pepi II of Egypt, who was at it for 94 years.

The shortest reign was that of Lady Jane Grey – just nine days in 1553. The world record is held by Dauphin Louis Antoine, who was King of France for only 15 minutes in 1830. He abdicated in favour of Henry V.

The nastiest royal parents were the early Georges: both hated their eldest sons. George II (1727–60) called his son 'the greatest beast in the whole world' and his wife Queen Caroline said as she died: 'At least I shall have one comfort . . . I shall never see that monster again.'

The worst royal husband was (of course) Henry VIII (1509–47), who beheaded two of his six wives and divorced two others. Chief rival is George IV (1820–30) who called for brandy after embracing his wife, Caroline. After a brief honeymoon he never lived with her as a husband.

The most eccentric king was the hapless George III (1760–1820), whose illness affected his brain. He would shake hands with an oak tree, thinking it was the King of Prussia.

The cruellest king was probably Henry V (1413–22). He once besieged Rouen in France until its inhabitants were so hungry that they 'ete doggys, they ete cattys, they ete mysse, horse and rattys'.

The oddest monarchs: Louis XIV of France (1643–1715) was born with a complete set of teeth; Anne Boleyn (wife of Henry VIII) had six fingers on her left hand, and Charles I (1625–49) was 4ft 8in tall.

The greediest king: There were lots, but King Henry I (1100–1135) paid for his greed. He perished after eating too many lampreys. (Lampreys? Oh, you know, a sort of eel with a sucker mouth. Do we have to tell you everything?)

LEFT-HANDERS
British left-handers

A list compiled specially for us by Shirley Read of Wallington, Surrey.

ROYALTY
George VI

WRITERS AND JOURNALISTS
Elkan Allan
Michael Barsley
Tim Crawley-Boevey (Editor of *Which?*)
James Green
Compton Mackenzie
Tim Matthews
Peter Scott
Ronald Searle
Richard Whitmore
Godfrey Winn

SPORTS PERSONALITIES
Athletics
Steve Ovett

Bowls
Loraine Hawes (British Ladies' Champion)
Boxing
Henry Cooper
Jim Watt
Cricket
Ken Barrington
Denis Compton
David Gower
John Steele (Leics)
Colin Dredge (Somerset)
Tennis
Mark Cox
Ann Hayden Jones
Bill Knight
Kay Stammers (Menzies) (Wimbledon singles and doubles champion, late 1930s)
Roger Taylor

THEATRE AND ENTERTAINMENT
Elizabeth Allen
Jeremy Brett
Brenda Bruce
Charlie Chaplin
Peter Cook
Michael Crawford
Peter Egan
Marianne Faithfull
Michael Flanders
Rex Harrison
Mary Hopkin
Jessie Matthews
Paul McCartney
Magnus Magnusson
Michael Parkinson
Eric Porter
Esther Rantzen
Leonard Rossiter
William Rushton

Terence Stamp
Jack Train
Ben Warris
Moray Watson
Richard Wattis
Kenneth Williams

POLITICIANS
Aneurin Bevan
James Callaghan
Roy Jenkins
Harold Macmillan

MURDERERS
Jack the Ripper

Items most in demand for left-handed people

'Anything Left-handed' is a shop in Beak Street, London, specializing in, you've guessed it, goods for left-handed people. Here is their list of best-sellers:

Butterfly can opener
Potato peeler
Bread knife
Nail scissors
Kitchen scissors
Osmiroid fountain pen
Address book with left-handed index
Left-handed ruler (measurements reading from right to left)
Children's left-handed paper scissors

No. 1 present for the left-handed bride-to-be: an electric iron with the flex connected to the left hand side of the iron.

Left-handed foreigners

There must be millions of them, but we're really only interested in Brits in this book. Oh well, if you insist . . .

Leonardo da Vinci
Kim Novak
Julius Caesar
President Gerald Ford
Napoleon

LEISURE
So what do we do with our spare time?
General Household Survey: Social Trends

The annual average percentage of people engaging in selected activities in 1980 was as follows. To be precise, they did them in the four weeks before they were interviewed. Curiously, 64 per cent of men had been out for a cultural drink but only two per cent had stayed home knitting.

	men	women
Open-air activities		
Seaside	7	7
Country	4	4
Parks	3	4
Entertainment/social/cultural activities		
Going out for a drink	64	45
Going out for a meal	40	40
Dancing	12	15
Going to the cinema	11	10
Visiting historic buildings	9	9
Theatre/opera/ballet	4	5
Amateur music/drama	4	3
Museums/art galleries	3	3
Fairs/amusement arcades	2	2
Attending leisure classes	1	2

Home-based activities		
Listening to records/tapes	66	62
Reading books	52	61
House repairs/DIY	53	23
Gardening	49	38
Games of skill	20	15
Needlework/knitting	2	51
Hobbies	11	3

LETTERS TO FAMOUS PEOPLE

Young Jonathan Gibbs, who lives in Cricklewood, north London, wrote to 16 well-known people and asked them to come and give a talk at his school. Only two agreed to speak, which was very good of them, while all of the others, except for three, did at least reply, even though they refused.

This is Jonathan's own list of how they replied:

Barry Took – The first person to say yes to my letters. A charming and witty writer and speaker.

Cyril Fletcher – Naturally comes second in my list since he was my second guest. The terseness of his sentences was more than adequately compensated by the meeting itself.

Spike Milligan – Spike replied very quickly, but he was in Australia at the time proposed for his talk.

Arthur Askey – The veteran comic had to decline my invitation, not because of ill health, but because he was touring the country in a farce at the time.

Henry Root – Mr Root is himself an infamous letter writer. I asked him to speak to my society on anything except 'the socio-economic structure of Southern Italy'. Unfortunately, since his chosen subject would have been 'the socio-economic structure of Southern Italy', Mr Root had to decline.

Richard Stilgoe – He sent me an Australian postcard on which he apologized for not being able to come since he would be returning to Australia at the time of the talk.

Harry Secombe – Sir Harry wrote a very kind letter to me, explaining that for the next few months he would be out of London.

Richard Briers – He sent me a postcard on which he said that he could only attend charity functions.

Tim Brooke-Taylor – Tim had commitments like writing a book and completing a television series.

Roger Moore – I received a signed photograph of 007 without any letter, so perhaps he will drop in one day.

Those are all my personally signed letters. I also have:
   a letter from Mrs Barry Norman
   a letter from Mrs Thatcher's personal secretary
   a letter from Esther Rantzen (signed in her absence)

The people who have never replied are as follows:
   Michael Bentine
   Paul Daniels
   Kenny Everett

LICENCES:
TV LICENCE FEES
British fees since 1922

The separate fee for radio was abolished in 1971.

	monochrome	colour	radio
1 November 1922	—	—	10s (50p)
1 June 1946	£2	—	£1
1 June 1954	£3	—	£1
1 August 1957	£4	—	£1
1 August 1965	£5	—	£1/5s (£1.25)
1 January 1968	£5	£10	£1/5s (£1.25)
1 January 1969	£6	£11	£1/5s (£1.25)
1 July 1971	£7	£12	
1 April 1975	£8	£18	
29 July 1977	£9	£21	

	monochrome	colour
25 November 1978	£10	£25
24 November 1979	£12	£34
1 December 1981	£15	£46

European fees, 1981

	monochrome	colour
Denmark	£43	£72
Sweden	£48	£63
Belgium	£43	£62
Norway	£50	£62
Switzerland	£60	£60
Finland	£34/£25	£59/£50
Austria	£57	£57
United Kingdom	£15	£46
France	£26	£40
Ireland	£24	£39
West Germany	£37	£37
Italy	£19	£35
Holland	£31	£31

Britain moved up three places in the European licence fee league table, from eleventh to eighth. All countries except Norway, Sweden, Denmark and Britain carry advertising on some services supported by the licence fee. Finland's system is two-tier, the higher amount payable in two-network regions. Seven countries charge a fee for radio only.

LIFE EXPECTANCY

Government Actuary's Department

expectation of life	males 1978	females 1978
From birth	70.0	76.1
From age 1 year	70.1	76.0
10 years	61.3	67.2
15 years	56.4	62.3
20 years	51.6	57.4

expectation of life	males 1978	females 1978
30 years	42.1	47.6
40 years	32.6	38.0
45 years	28.0	33.3
50 years	23.6	28.8
60 years	15.8	20.4
65 years	12.5	16.5
70 years	9.7	12.9
75 years	7.4	9.8
80 years	5.6	7.1

In 1901, the life expectancy of a male baby was 48 years and a female 51 years. The improving health of the population has greatly increased everyone's chance of reaching an older age group.

LIKES

Harry Fieldhouse: Over 21 Magazine

Well, we had Hates earlier on. You didn't notice Hates? Oh, they were very good. So now some Likes.

Physical attributes men imagine women admire most about them

		%
1	Muscular chest and shoulders	21
2	Muscular arms	18
3	Penis	15
4	Tallness	13
5	Flat stomach	9
6	Slimness	7
7	Hair texture	4
8	Buttocks	4
9	Eyes	4
10	Long legs	3
11	Neck	2

Physical attributes women really admire most about men

		%
1	Buttocks (small and sexy)	39
2	Slimness	15
3	Flat stomach	13
4	Eyes	11
5	Long legs	6
6	Tallness	5
7	Hair	5
8	Neck	3
9	Penis	2
10	Muscular chest and shoulders	1
11	Muscular arms	0

LITERATURE
Literary lacunae

The *Literary Review* asked an august selection of contributors to name the books that ought to have been written, but had not, or those which had been written but which were now unavailable. Writers, and their suggestions, included the following:

Auberon Waugh – an annual indexed summary of all the books published in Britain, with a summary both of the plot and the critical reception to the book.

Brigid Brophy – the novels of Shena Mackay, now out of print: *Toddler on the Run*, *Dust Falls on Eugene Schlumberger*, *Music Upstairs*, *Old Crow* and *An Advent Calendar*.

Tariq Ali – *Our Own People* by Elizabeth Poretsky and *A Non-Jewish Jew and Other Essays* by Isaac Deutscher.

Edna O'Brien – *Aspects of Love in Western Society* by Suzanne Lilar.

Enoch Powell – 'I have for some time been looking for a good English and Hebrew dictionary.'

Kingsley Amis – two books: an updated and improved Thesaurus, and a directory of English writers from the beginnings to the present day, complete with all their works.

Lindsay Anderson – *The Journal Intime of Henri-Frederic Amiel*, once in print, but now out of it, and H. R. Milar's *The Dreamland Express* ditto. Never published in this country: *Pappy*, the biography of film director John Ford by his grandson Dan Ford.

Anthony Powell – a biography should be written of Dawson Turner (1775–1858), antiquarian, botanist and patron of the arts. 'Someone was writing a life of him about fifty years ago, but nothing came of it.'

Sir Alfred Ayer – Lecky's *History of European Morals*.

Marina Warner – Both *Mimesis* by Erich Auerbach and *The Tongue Set Free* by Elias Canetti should be back in print.

Literary laziness: the great unread

Philip Howard, the Literary Editor of *The Times*, lists some of those books which everybody agrees to be great and influential; everybody quotes from; we are all influenced by; but, although we would die rather than admit it, very few of us actually read . . .

The Book of Job
Finnegan's Wake by James Joyce
The Book Of Common Prayer
The Divine Comedy by Dante Alighieri
Don Quixote de la Mancha by Miguel de Cervantes Saavedra
The Sonnets of William Shakespeare
The Georgics by Vergil
Das Kapital by Karl Marx
Pantagruel by François Rabelais
The Iliad by Homer

LIVERY COMPANIES

The Livery Companies of the City of London are so called after the adoption by their members of distinctive styles of dress in the fourteenth century. The twelve Great Companies, in order of precedence, are:

The Mercers

The Grocers

The Drapers

The Fishmongers

The Goldsmiths

The Skinners

The Merchant Taylors

The Haberdashers

The Salters

The Ironmongers

The Vintners

The Clothworkers

LOCAL AUTHORITY EXPENDITURE IN UK, 1980-81

H.M. Treasury: Social Trends

	£ million
Education	10 700
Environmental services	3 582
Law, order, and protective services	2 649
Housing	2 561
Roads and transport	2 341
Health and personal social services	1 943
Libraries, museums and the arts	320
Trade and industry, energy, agriculture, food and forestry	217
Employment services	73
Other public services	44
	24 430

LONDON PLACES

As we have all those Irish, Scottish and Welsh lists, it seemed only fair to give London a few mentions.

Molly Parkin's favourite London places

Few social occasions in the capital are complete without the presence of novelist Molly Parkin and her daughters. She came originally from Wales but is now more than qualified to give a list of the London places into which any self-respecting socialite should attempt to gain entry at all costs. Some of the hot spots she mentions require only a carrier bag and a shopping list. Others are a touch more exclusive:

1 **The Screen on the Green** – the Islington cinema
2 **Langan's Brasserie** – the perennially successful celebrity diner
3 **Foxtrot Oscars** – the Chelsea restaurant
4 **The Chelsea Arts Club**
5 **The Zanzibar** – the Covent Garden bar. 'One of my daughters is a waitress there.'
6 **C & A**
7 **Sainsbury's**
8 **The Arts Council Bookshop** – in Long Acre, Covent Garden
9 **Ricci Burns'** hairdressing salon
10 **Ronnie Scott's**
11 **Rose Lewis** bra shop, Knightsbridge. 'It's well-known by some funny people. It's for sensualists.'
12 **Cornucopia,** Victoria – 'It sells the best old clothes. You meet someone there you met in Venice six months ago.'
13 **The Café de Paris** – 'We go to the tea dances there and we go late at night. It's like the Streatham Locarno or Hammersmith Palais – we all come in as Hollywood.'
14 **The Cottesloe Theatre** – at the National Theatre. 'My other daughter works there.'
15 **The Gay Hussar** – the Soho restaurant. 'But only at lunch when Victor's there.'

16 **On the bus** – 'Well, we've all taken to the buses nowadays.'
17 **Waitrose** in the King's Road
18 **The Embassy** – 'It's the only nightclub I enjoy, but you have to know people there.'

London places Molly Parkin does not go to

But what about the places you wouldn't be seen dead in, Molly? 'I don't go to places that I don't like, so I don't know enough about them to make a long list.' She did, however, come up with a few suggestions. They could of course be read as recommendations. Place where you can *avoid* seeing M. Parkin . . .

1 **Marks and Spencer** – 'They're so sensible. I think C&A are much better.'
2 **Jaeger**
3 **Any estate agent** – 'They're all so snotty to you.'
4 **Harrods**
5 **Boots** – 'Too depressing . . .'
6 **Habitat** – '. . . horrible . . .'
7 **Any bank** – '. . . We always use the chequepoint machines.'
8 **Nightclubs** – 'I don't go out to nightclubs except for the Embassy. I particularly don't like Tokyo Joe's; it's full of Hooray Henries.'
9 **No Chinese or Indian restaurants** – 'Except the ones in Bradford and Leeds, specially Bradford, which are fabulous.'
10 **Laura Ashley**

Capital entertainment

According to the readers of the London *Standard*'s Ad Lib column, these are London's finest cocktail bars, music pubs, restaurants and nightclubs.

LONDON'S BEST COCKTAIL BARS
 1 *Rumours*
 2 *Peppermint Park*

3 *Coconut Grove*
4 *Zanzibar*
5 *Blushes*
6 *Lazy Toad*
7 *Sloanes*
8 *Beachcomber*
9 *Kettner's*
10 *Chez Solange*

Note: Three of the first four are in Covent Garden. Since the district also harbours the *Café des Amis du Vin*, where the country's most wicked champagne cocktail (complete with passion-fruit juice) is served, it is clearly the best part of town in which to get drunk in style.

LONDON'S BEST MUSIC PUBS
1 *The Hope and Anchor*, Islington
2 *The Golden Lion*, Fulham
3 *The Bridge House*, Canning Town
4 *The Greyhound*, Fulham
5 *The Hog's Grunt*, Cricklewood
6 *The Horseshoe*, Tottenham Court Road
7 *The Half Moon*, Putney
8 *The Half Moon*, Herne Hill
9 *Dingwalls*, Camden Lock
10 *The Cartoon*, Croydon

LONDON'S BEST RESTAURANTS
1 *The Hard Rock Café*
2 *Langan's Brasserie*
3 *McDonald's*
4 *Maxwell's*
5 *Joe Allen*
6 *Strikes*
7 *The Ritz*
8 *Meridiana*
9 *Chicago Pizza Pie Factory*
10 *Porter's*

LONDON'S BEST NIGHTSPOTS

1 *The Venue*, Victoria
2 *Stringfellow's*, Covent Garden
3 *The Embassy*, Mayfair
4 *The Lyceum*, The Strand
5 bed
6 *Ronnie Scott's*, Soho
7 *Peppermint Park*, Covent Garden
8 *Thursdays*, Kensington
9 *Legends*, Mayfair
10 *Le Beat Route*, Soho

For out-of-towners and adventurous travellers, *The Face* magazine recommends *The Ultrathèque* in Glasgow, *Hunter's* in Cardiff and *Sherry's* in Birmingham. Those in the know maintain that *Annabel's*, in Berkeley Square, is still the greatest of them all.

LORDS AND LADIES

In case you should ever be elevated, be careful how you conduct yourself. They're very strict about such things in the House of Lords. The House is composed of the following groups (February 1982):

Order of precedence

The Lord Chancellor (1)
Peers of The Blood Royal (4)
Archbishops (2)
Dukes (25)
Marquesses (28)
Earls (152)
Viscounts (103)
Barons and Scots Lords (492)
Peeresses in their own right (19)
Life Peers (288)
Life Peeresses (43)
Bishops (23)

Minor Lords

This is a list of kids who have become peers and are still under the age of 21.

	born
Rufus Arnold Alexis Keppel, tenth Earl of Albermarle	1965
Joseph Philip Sebastian Yorke, tenth Earl of Hardwicke	1971
Giles John Harry Goschen, fourth Viscount Goschen	1965
William Keith Mason, fourth Baron Blackford	1962
Clifton Hugh Lancelot de Verdon Wrottesley, sixth Baron Wrottesley	1968

LOST PROPERTY

London Transport

The Lost Property Office is a good indicator of changing human habits. The onetime glut of hats and gloves is gradually being superseded by credit cards, pocket calculators and expensive cameras, etc. Even the number of brollies has been halved in the last few years – the telescopic model being less easily mislaid if carried in a case or bag.

About 134 000 items are handed in annually of which about a third are restored to their owners.

Commonest articles, 1981

Handbags and purses	26 000
Umbrellas	24 000
Items of clothing	19 000
Books	14 000
Pairs of gloves	11 000
Cases and other bags	9 000
Odd gloves	2 000

Unusual articles

Among the many strange items handed in during recent years:

A pair of false teeth
A stuffed gorilla
A three-foot spanner
A box of glass eyes
A bed
A confidential list of the Queen's engagements
A complete ice-hockey kit
An artificial hand
A five-foot garden seat
A bag of human bones

MAGAZINES
Top 20 magazines and periodicals, 1981

Based on the certified circulation figures for the first half of 1981 published by the Audit Bureau of Circulation Ltd.

Average net sales per publishing day

Radio Times	3 545 763
TV Times	3 254 277
Woman's Weekly	1 580 257
Woman's Own	1 475 116
Woman	1 383 181
Woman's Realm	681 251
Family Circle	665 374
Woman & Home	648 314
Weekend	565 424
Puzzler	530 861
Living	502 412
Cosmopolitan	467 907
Good Housekeeping	368 766
Beauty & Skincare	353 086
Mayfair	351 464

Slimming	320 507
Exchange & Mart	313 399
Fiesta	294 008
Titbits	291 171
She	279 040

The Christmas issues of the *Radio Times* and the *TV Times* for 1981 both sold well over 8 million copies.

Business and professional journals

The top seller in this category was the C.P.S.A. (Civil Service) journal *Red Tape* with 217 246 copies.

Bottom of this category with a mere 378 copies (1980) was the *Anglo Russian and East European State Purchasing Review*.

MARKS & SPENCER

There were 255 Marks & Spencer stores in the UK as of the end of 1981. Here are their top ten selling lines in order of cash taken in 1981. The top ten for 1980 are shown in parentheses.

Marks & Spencer's top ten selling lines

1	Ladies' dresses	(Chicken)
2	Fruit, vegetables and salads	(Ladies' jumpers)
3	Ladies' skirts	(Ladies' skirts)
4	Men's trousers and jeans	(Ladies' trousers and jeans)
5	Cakes and desserts	(Men's trousers and jeans)
6	Poultry	(Ladies' dresses)
7	Meat and bacon	(Cakes and desserts)
8	Ladies' blouses	(Men's long-sleeved shirts)
9	Ladies' jumpers	(Ladies' long-sleeved blouses)
10	Pies, pizzas and pasta	(Pies and flans)

We seem to be eating less chicken but far more fruit and vegetables than before. Are ladies' jumpers going out of fashion? Marks & Spencer point out that they change their product groupings regularly and that this can affect placings to some extent. Also the above list is based on total cash taken. In terms of individual items sold, underwear would easily top the league. M & S sell over 100 million pairs of knickers every year.

MARRIAGE
Marriages in Great Britain, 1979
Offices of Population Censuses and Surveys

	thousands
First marriage for both partners	270
First marriage for one partner only:	
bachelor/divorced woman	33
bachelor/widow	3
spinster/divorced man	36
spinster/widower	3
Second (or later) marriage for both partners:	
both divorced	43
both widowed	8
divorced man/widow	5
divorced woman/widower	5
Total marriages -	406

MEDICINES
Top ten home medicines
Dr Vernon Coleman: The Home Pharmacy

1 Cough and cold remedies
2 Painkillers
3 Vitamins

4 Indigestion remedies
5 Germicides and antiseptics
6 Laxatives
7 Tonics
8 Rubs and linaments
9 Eye preparations
10 Foot care products

Headache remedies – the brand leaders

The Money Programme, BBC

		% market
1	Anadin	19
2	Disprin	15
3	Hedex	8
4	Phensic	7
5	Aspro	6

All in fact are variations on Paracetamol/Aspirin.

Women are more prone to headaches than men. There is a great deal of brand loyalty – people tend to stick with the product they *believe* does them good.

Top four cold remedies

1 Beecham's Powders
2 Lemsip
3 Night Nurse
4 Vick's Medinite

Scientifically unproven products that have made a lot of money

Carbolic Smokeball
Daffy's Elixir
Dr Bateman's pectoral drops
Dr Swayne's consumption cure
Samuel Lee's bilious pills
Widow Read's ointment for the Itch

MURDERERS
Britain's Top Ten murderers

When it comes to mass murder the British are a nation of pussycats. We have no one to compare with the German murderer Fritz Haarman who, in the years after the First World War, killed at least forty teenage boys and sold their bodies for meat. Nor can we match the speed of execution displayed by Charles Whitman; on 1 August 1966, the 25-year-old American student climbed to the top of the observation tower at the University of Texas and shot 46 passers-by before the police could shoot him.

The list of the ten most prolific British murderers – for which I am indebted to J. H. H. Gaute and Robin Odell's gruesome encyclopedia *The Murderer's Who's Who* – is as follows:

1 **Burke and Hare.** The two Edinburgh body-snatchers killed sixteen of their fellow-citizens and made a handsome profit supplying their corpses to dissection rooms at the city's medical schools. William Burke was hanged on 28 January 1829 after his partner had turned King's Evidence.

2 **Mary Ann Cotton.** Mary Ann proved that the female is indeed deadlier than the male by establishing the British solo record at a minimum of 14 or 15 victims. Husbands, lovers, children, stepchildren, none were safe from this obsessive poisoner who was finally hanged at Durham gaol in 1873.

3 **Dr William Palmer.** He was another fond of removing his nearest and dearest, this time in an attempt to evade bankruptcy by collecting on relatives' insurance. When creditors pressed him too hard, Palmer poisoned them as well. Palmer's trial in 1856 made legal history; such was the public feeling against him that the 'Palmer Act' was passed enabling an accused person to be tried in London if he was unlikely to get a fair trial in his home county.

4 **Peter Sutcliffe.** The 'Yorkshire Ripper' is an all-too-recent addition to the list. He raped, killed and mutilated at least

thirteen young women and is suspected of a number of other murders both in northern England and on the continent. Finally caught after a massive police search which has since itself become the subject of an official investigation.

5 **John George Haigh.** Whereas Sutcliffe might well be placed higher in the list, Haigh – who confessed to nine 'Acid Bath Murders' – may deserve a lower position; three of his victims are thought to have been the products of his warped imagination. Haigh disposed of the bodies by leaving them in vats of sulphuric acid, having first had a drink of their blood. He was finally executed at Wandsworth prison on 10 August 1949.

6 **Peter Manuel.** When the Glasgow police took Manuel in for questioning about a minor burglary in early 1958 he gave them rather more evidence than they had bargained for, confessing to two triple murders and two individual killings. At his trial Manuel conducted his own defence, but was unable to prevent being sent to the gallows. Eight was almost certainly a very conservative estimate of the number of murders he actually committed.

7 **Amelia Elizabeth Dyer.** This lady, the 'Reading Baby Farmer', murdered a minimum of seven, and possibly many more, children, all of whom had been boarding at her house in Reading where she 'looked after' unwanted babies. Executed in 1896, Dyer is said to have returned as a ghost to haunt her warder at Newgate.

7 Equal with Dyer is **John Reginald Halliday Christie.** The infamous inhabitant of 10 Rillington Place raped and murdered six women during the 1940s and early 50s, perhaps in an attempt to compensate for the sexual inadequacy that had earned him the nickname of Reggie No-Dick as a young man. He also confessed to the murder of a seventh woman, his neighbour Mrs Evans, for which her husband was hanged in 1950. Christie followed him to the scaffold three years later.

9 **Frederick Bayley Deeming.** Two wives and four children ended up buried beneath Mr Deeming's hearths in both Liverpool and Sydney, Australia, whither he had emigrated in 1891. He was executed the following year before a crowd of 10000.

10 **Dr Thomas Neill Cream.** The 'Lambeth Poisoner' claimed at least five victims before falling victim to his own desire for publicity; he offered to name the guilty man in return for £300 000; the police arrested him and discovered the information for free. As he was executed in 1892 he is alleged to have shouted, 'I am Jack the . . .'

Jack the Ripper. The most famous murderer of them all tore apart five victims, thus failing to make the gruesome Top Ten above, but firmly establishing himself as the most notorious criminal ever to have escaped detection. A list of the men suspected of the killings of five East End prostitutes in 1888 would include Messrs Deeming and Cream above, The Duke of Clarence, Dr Alexander Pedachenko, Dr Stanley, Sir William Gull, J. K. Stephen, and a barrister turned schoolmaster called Montague John Druitt, not to mention a host of Freemasons, doctors and slaughtermen.

The ten most famous
unsolved British murders

The Ripper murders must be placed at the top of this list. Here are the next nine:

2 **The Croydon Poisonings.** Three members of the same family died from arsenic poisoning between April 1928 and March 1929. The only surviving member of the family, Mrs Grace Duff, was suspected of the murders, but survived uncharged to the age of 87.

3 **Gorse Hall Murder.** On 1 November 1909 someone killed George Storrs, a prosperous builder, at his Cheshire home. Despite the fact that the killer was seen by several people, and that a suspect was eventually tried and found 'not guilty', the case remains a mystery; a classic country house murder.

4 **The Brighton Trunk Cases.** In 1933 two bodies were found decomposing in trunks in Brighton. One, minus head and legs, at the station; the other in a lodging house. One Tony

Mancini was tried, but sensationally acquitted, for the second murder. As for the first, the identities of both murderer and victim have never been discovered.

5 **The Lucan Case.** Did Lord Lucan murder his children's nanny and severely injure his wife? Did he kill himself soon after, or is he still in hiding, protected, perhaps, by members of his tight-knit aristocratic circle of friends? After the best part of a decade, the questions are still no nearer to being answered.

6 **The Hammersmith Nudes Murders.** Six prostitutes were killed between February 1964 and February 1965 – all were found nude. The murders ceased after a man, still unnamed, committed suicide, leaving a note saying he was 'unable to stand the strain any longer'.

7 **The Chevis Case.** On 21 June 1931 Lieutenant Hubert Chevis died in his married quarters at Aldershot camp after eating poisoned partridge. His wife was ill, but recovered. On the day of Chevis's funeral his father received a telegram from Dublin, signed J. Hartigan, saying 'Hooray, hooray, hooray'. It was followed by another which read, 'It is a mystery they will never solve', and they never have.

8 **The Luard Case.** When General Charles Luard's wife was killed in 1908, public suspicion centred upon him, even though he was known to love her dearly and could prove that he was nowhere near the scene of the crime at the time when it was committed. So upset was Luard by the accusations that he committed suicide by jumping in front of a train. His wife's killer was never traced.

9 **The Oakes Case.** Sir Harry Oakes started life as an American gold prospector. He ended it as a Baronet, battered to death in his house in the Bahamas on 8 July 1943. The murder weapon was never found, nor were the bloody hand-prints around the room in which the body was found ever explained; nor, for that matter, was the fact that the corpse had been partly burned and feathers scattered all over it. The Duke of Windsor was governing the Bahamas at the time, and there are question marks over the way he conducted the investigation into the affair. Why, for example, did he ignore the island police, but call in detectives from Miami instead?

10   **The Bingham Poisonings.** Edith Bingham was put on trial in October 1911 for the murder of her father, sister and brother by poisoning, despite the fact that there was no evidence to show that she had ever possessed any poison, let alone administered it. She was acquitted, and the mystery was never solved.

MUSEUMS

Attendances at museums and art galleries

British Tourist Authority

	thousands	
ART GALLERIES	*1971*	*1980*
National Gallery	1 859	2 618
Tate Gallery	936	1 331
Royal Academy	250	1 062
National Portrait Gallery	513	449
Hayward Gallery	137	186
Scottish National Gallery	241	342
Serpentine Gallery	55	189
MUSEUMS		
British Museum	2 680	3 880
Science Museum	1 942	5 790
Natural History Museum	1 576	2 385
Victoria and Albert	2 034	1 723
Imperial War Museum	557	1 454
National Railway Museum, York	—	1 335
National Maritime Museum	1 591	1 145
Royal Scottish Museum	534	630
Geological Museum	345	542
National Museum of Wales	383	351
Welsh Folk Museum	185	278

The British Tourist Authority estimated that in 1980 galleries in Great Britain received 53.5 million visitors.

NAMES
Christian names from The Times

Based on researches through *The Times* birth columns by a *Times* reader, Margaret Brown from York.

name	number in 1981	1980 position
BOYS		
1 James*	229	(1)
2 William	183	(3)
3 Alexander	134	(2)
4 Thomas	131	(4)
5 Edward	128	(6)
6 John	127	(5)
7 Charles	118	(7)
8 David	99	(8)
9 Nicholas	82	(14)
10 Michael	77	(11)

* James has been top of the charts for eighteen years, but there were fourteen fewer babies of that name announced in *The Times* last year than the year before. Names that fell from the list were Robert and Richard.

name	number in 1981	1980 position
GIRLS		
1 Elizabeth*	122	(1)
2 Louise	98	(2)
3 Jane	80	(3)
4 Sarah	79	(5)
5 Charlotte	70	(11)
6 Victoria	67	(7)
7 Mary	66	(4)
8 Katherine	60	(9)
9 Alexandra	57	(10)
10 Lucy	52	(12)

* Elizabeth has also been a perennial favourite, although both she and Louise have lost ground to the competition during the past year. Clare and Alice have dropped out. Can we expect a new entry from Diana next time?

Alphabetical list of some people best known by their initials

W. H. Auden – Wystan Hugh
H. E. Bates – Herbert Ernest
R. D. Blackmore – Richard Doddridge
G. K. Chesterton – Gilbert Keith
A. J. Cronin – Archibald Joseph
e. e. Cummings – Ernest Estlin
R. F. Delderfield – Ronald Frederick
T. S. Elliot – Thomas Stearns
E. M. Forster – Edward Morgan
W. S. Gilbert – William Schwenk
A. P. Herbert – Alan Patrick
A. E. Houseman – Alfred Edward
D. H. Lawrence – David Herbert
T. E. Lawrence – Thomas Edward
C. S. Lewis – Clive Staples
A. A. Milne – Alan Alexander
L. M. Montgomery – Lucy Maud
H. H. Munro – Hugh Hector
J. B. Priestley – John Boynton
W. H. Smith – William Henry
C. P. Snow – Charles Percy
P. L. Travers – Pamela Lyndon
H. G. Wells – Herbert George
T. H. White – Terence Hanbury
P. G. Wodehouse – Pelham Grenville
F. W. Woolworth – Frank Winfield
P. C. Wren – Percival Christopher
W. B. Yeats – William Butler

This list was compiled and researched by J. A. Twelves – John Anthony (father) – and H. L. Twelves – Helen Louise (daughter) of Cheadle, Cheshire.

22 renowned people
known by a middle name

It's surprising the number of politicians not known by their first name, so says Paul Donnelley of Essex who compiled this list.

1	John *Michael* Brearley	cricketer
2	Cedric *Keith* Simpson	pathologist
3	Alan *Ross* McWhirter	writer
4	Edward *Hunter* Davies	writer
5	Sir James *Harold* Wilson	prime minister
6	Leonard *James* Callaghan	prime minister
7	James *Ramsay* MacDonald	prime minister
8	James *Keir* Hardie	politician
9	John *Enoch* Powell	politician
10	Maurice *Harold* Macmillan	prime minister
11	Arthur *Neville* Chamberlain	prime minister
12	Joseph *Austen* Chamberlain	politician
13	James *David* Graham Niven	actor
14	Sir Robert *Anthony* Eden	prime minister
15	Thomas *Malcolm* Muggeridge	writer
16	Sir Arthur *John* Gielgud	actor
17	Sir Richard Edward *Geoffrey* Howe	politician
18	Rita *Gemma* Craven	actress
19	James *Paul* McCartney	singer-songwriter
20	Stanley *Michael* Bailey Hailwood	motorcyclist
21	Graham *Anthony* Richard Lock	cricketer
22	Michael *Colin* Cowdrey	cricketer

NEWSPAPERS

National newspapers

Based on the certified circulation figures for the second half of 1981 published by the Audit Bureau of Circulation Ltd.

Average net sales per publishing day:

DAILIES

1	*Sun*	4 136 927
2	*Daily Mirror*	3 413 785
3	*Daily Express*	2 196 492
4	*Daily Mail*	1 887 051
5	*Daily Star*	1 508 047
6	*Daily Telegraph*	1 342 007
7	*Guardian*	397 708
8	*Times*	297 787
9	*Financial Times*	197 742
10	*Sporting Life*	64 087

SUNDAYS

1	*News of the World*	4 236 715
2	*Sunday Mirror*	3 786 454
3	*Sunday People*	3 629 687
4	*Sunday Express*	2 993 763
5	*Sunday Times*	1 363 640
6	*Sunday Telegraph*	916 644
7	*Observer*	886 985

The largest regional daily circulation was the *Daily Record* (Scotland) with 736 004.

The largest circulation evening newspapers were:

1	*Standard* (London)	569 305
2	*Manchester Evening News*	313 479
3	*Birmingham Evening Mail*	302 023

The *Sunday Mail* (Scotland) has by far the largest circulation of the regional Sundays: 748 891.

Newspaper headlines

When Frank Peters left the *Northern Echo*, Darlington, in January 1982, he arranged for the news paragraphs on the front page of the 16th January issue to spell out a special message for one of his senior colleagues, Mr Pifer. Can you read his parting shot to Mr Pifer?

Freeze ending

The big freeze is coming to an end. A slow thaw is expected to gain momentum in the next few days and temperatures will climb to 7°C over the weekend.

Up and up

RAF search-and-rescue helicopters have flown 187 mercy missions since the blizzards and freeze-up began.

Child-saver

The Government announced yesterday it would give a £450 000 grant to the NSPCC over the next three years – to save children's lives.

'Keep off'

The Government yesterday blocked takeover bids for the Royal Bank of Scotland by both the Hongkong and Shanghai Banking Corporation and the Standard Chartered Bank.

Plane 'iced up'

A witness saw ice crusted on the airliner which crashed in Washington on Wednesday killing 78 people, a US investigator said yesterday.

Inflation steady

Britain's annual inflation rate remained at 12% in December, the same as November, according to the Retail Price Index.

Feathered find

Mrs Marie Tyler, of Sutton Coldfield, who lost a gold ring six weeks ago, believes that one of the birds she feeds found it and put it on her back garden bird table.

Everybody out

Workers walked out on strike when Mrs Thatcher visited Kellogg's giant breakfast cereal plant at Trafford Park, Manchester, yesterday.

Rolling on

Two high-rolling gamblers from Las Vegas were thought to be on their way to London after winning £20 000 at roulette in a Northampton casino.

Newspaper howlers

Frank Peters, who is now a sub-editor on *The Times* in London, collected the following specimens over a period of 30 years of subbing on *The Northern Echo*, Darlington, and the *Scottish Daily Mail*, Edinburgh.

1 An inquest was opened yesterday and adjourned until today at Stoke-on-Trent on the body of a Meteor jet pilot who crashed at Newcastle-under-Lyme on Friday within 100 yards of his home to enable identification to be definitely established.

2 Miss Power is a 17 year old calculating machine operator.

3 The Coroner expressed thanks to everyone who had taken part in the tragedy.

4 'He was trying to put the flames out. I pulled him away, warmed the rest of the family and then called the fire brigade.'

5 'He is in bed. A British woman doctor is with him. I am not authorized to give any further information.'

6 Mrs K.J., an Aberdeen fish filleter was jailed for four months at Aberdeen Sheriff Court yesterday when she admitted carrying out an abortion on a shop assistant. (All in a day's work!)

7 Mrs Violent Kray, mother of the Kray twins.

8 Cheerful lady companion required in Bath.

9 A 21-year-old Ugandan bank clerk who felt inadequate tried to commit suicide three times before succeeding.

10 Councillor Bill Pritchard suggested that Scarborough had done nothing about a pool until they were forced into it.

11 re ad in third para 'mild applause greeted Sir Henry' substituting 'mild' for 'wild'.

12 The English seldom refuse a drink though only an insignificant minority appreciate good wind.

13 For 'real admiral' read 'rear admiral'.

14 A 74-year-old widow has filed a suit against a Los Angeles school of dancing for the recovery of £9000 she claims she paid for 2800 hours of lessons which failed to make her the gifted danger they promised.

15 A spider found in a bunch of bananas at Bridlington was examined by an expert and found to be a banana spider.

16 A diesel train struck the buggers at Forster Station.

17 Newton Aycliffe social centre requires a casual door steward.

18 South Shields Watch Committee agreed to give P.C. Mitchell £15 to replace his damaged watch. (ad hoc!)

19 Please read: 'he got into bed with her and she told him to go away.' This substitutes 'away' for 'ahead'.

20 She is 34 years old, 5ft 10ins, plump, and with shoulder length blue eyes.

And some headlines:

1 **MOTHER OF FOUR FORGED BANKNOTES**

2 **TEN HOURS ADRIFT ON TWO SUGAR LUMPS**

3 A pair of adjacent headlines of some 20 years ago:

WE CAN COMPETE	**TRAIN KILLS**
WITH ROAD HAULAGE	**LORRY DRIVER**
SAYS DR BEECHING	**ON CROSSING**

NUDISM

British nudist beaches

Ardeer Shore	(Stevenson, Strathclyde)
Brighton East Beach	(Brighton, Sussex)
Cleat's Shore	(Isle of Arran, Strathclyde)
Fairlight Cove	(Hastings, Sussex)
Fraisethorpe Sands	(Bridlington, Humberside)
Gunton Sands	(Lowestoft, Suffolk)
Leysdown East Beach	(Isle of Sheppey, Kent)
Longrock Beach	(Whitstable, Kent)

ODDS

Here's a list of the chances of an assortment of things happening to you, beginning at the top with the least likely:

	one chance in –
That you will win the pools	22 000 000
That you will be struck by lightning this year	2 000 000
That you will die in an air disaster	100 000
That you will die on the operating table	40 000
That you will die at birth	12 500
That you will be killed driving a car	4 000
That you will die on a motor cycle	500
That you will die from smoking more than 20 cigarettes a day	200
That you will be admitted to a mental hospital	133
That you will be burgled during the year	50
That you will be divorced some time in your life	3

You may like to contemplate the fact that the chance of being divorced is about the same as the chance that it will rain in London today.

OPEN UNIVERSITY

OU Digest of Statistics

Educational qualifications already attained by all registered students on entry to an Open University course, 1980.

type of qualification	%
No qualifications	7
1 or more CSE, RSA or SLC	3
1–4 GCE 'O' levels/SCE 'O' grades	9
5 or more GCE 'O' levels/SCE 'O' grades	12
1 'A' level/SCE 'H' grade	5
2 'A' levels or more/SCE 'H' grades	12
ONC/OND	4

HNC/HND	9
Teacher's certificate	25
University diploma	8
University first degree	6
Total students %	100
Thousands	61

Notice how many teachers there are, and how many have already been to a university. Further education seems to be for the further educated.

PAINTERS
Top portrait painters

The Top Ten portrait artists, compiled by the National Portrait Gallery:

1 Francis Bacon
2 David Hockney
3 Lucien Freud
4 Bryan Organ
5 Rodrigo Moynihan
6 Lawrence Gowing
7 Sir William Coldstream
8 Peter Blake
9 Carel Weight
10 Ruskin Spear

PAINTINGS
Sotheby's of London's world record prices for individual artists, 1981

£

460 000	Fernand Léger: *Les Arbres dans les Maisons*
320 000	Alfred Sisley: *La Seine à Argenteuil*
270 000	Jean-Etienne Liotard: *The painter's son at breakfast*

185 000	Dante Gabriel Rossetti: *The Damsel of the Sanct Grail*
170 000	Caspar David Friedrich: *A mountain peak with drifting clouds*
138 000	Johan Heinrich Zoffany: *Colonel Blair with his Family and an Ayah*
120 000	Raoul Dufy: *La Plage au Havre*
105 000	Washington Allston: *Hermia and Helena*
90 000	Giacomo Balla: *Velo vi Vedova e Paesaggio*
90 000	Ernest Ludwig Kirchner: *Olympia*

The above list comprises only paintings sold in the London salerooms.

PAINTS
Bedroom colours

In a recent poll conducted for Crown Paints, the following order of preference emerged in the choice of colour schemes for British bedrooms:

white	cream
pink	beige
blue	purple
green	lilac
brown	black
yellow	red

In 76% of the households consulted, the women had chosen the colours rather than the men. Could that be the reason that white 'for purity' was 26 times as popular as the more exotic black or red?

Dulux best-selling paint colours

I.C.I. compiles its own table of Top Ten colours for its Dulux range. Here's the 1981 list:

Dulux Gloss

1. Brilliant White
2. Black
3. Magnolia
4. Spice
5. Muffin
6. Buttermilk
7. Conker
8. Peppercorn
9. Bamboo
10. Buckingham (dark green)

Dulux Vinyl Matt Emulsion

1. Brilliant White
2. Magnolia
3. Buttermilk
4. Muffin
5. Almond Blossom
6. Cameo (ochre)
7. Sandalwood
8. Bamboo
9. Siesta (pale peach)
10. Country Clover and Summer Blue

PARKINSON APPEARANCES

If you've ever watched a Parkinson show and thought 'I'm sure I've seen this person before', you were probably right. Welcome guests have a habit of returning to the show at regular intervals. The most frequent chatterers (up to the end of 1981) have been:

1. Equal: **Spike Milligan** and **Jonathan Miller,** with seven appearances each.
3. **Billy Connolly,** five appearances.
4. Equal: **Robert Morley** and **Kenneth Williams,** four appearances each.
6. **Peter Ustinov,** three appearances.

The record for the most appearances on a single Parkinson programme goes to the Australian humourist Barry Humphries; on the Parkinson show of 30 January 1982 he made separate appearances as himself, Sir Les Patterson and as Dame Edna Everage.

A few days previously Kenneth Griffiths, the Welsh actor and maker of documentaries, set a new record for uninterrupted speech by taking ten minutes over the answer to a single question.

PARKS

Parks, grounds and gardens attracting more than 100 000 visitors, 1980

British Tourist Authority

Royal Botanic Gardens, Kew	991 200
Royal Botanic Gardens, Edinburgh	592 600
Royal Horticultural Society Garden, Wisley	411 500
Dunham Massey, Cheshire	300 000
Compton Acres Gardens, Poole	300 000
Glasgow Botanic Gardens	250 000
Temple Newsham House, Leeds	200 000
Stourhead, Wiltshire	186 400
Culzean Castle Grounds, Strathclyde	184 200
Kilverstone Wildlife Park, Thetford	178 000
Tatton Park, Knutsford	177 100
Bicton Gardens, East Budleigh	165 000
Lotherton Hall, near Leeds	150 000
Knebworth, Hertfordshire	141 400
Sheffield Park Garden	138 700
Polesden Lacey, near Dorking	108 000

PARLIAMENT

Social and educational comparison of British Cabinets

W. L. Gutsman: British Political Elite

date	PM	party	size	aristocrats	middle class	working class	public school any	Eton	university any	Oxbridge
Aug 1895	Salisbury	Con	19	8	11	—	16	9	15	14
Jul 1902	Balfour	Con	19	9	10	—	16	9	14	13
Dec 1905	Campbell-Bannerman	Lib	19	7	11	1	11	3	14	12
Jul 1914	Asquith	Lib	19	6	12	1	11	3	15	13
Jan 1919	Lloyd George	Coal	21	3	17	1	12	2	13	8
Nov 1922	Bonar Law	Con	16	8	8	—	14	8	13	13
Jan 1924	Macdonald	Lab	19	3	5	11	8	—	6	6
Nov 1924	Baldwin	Con	21	9	12	—	21	7	16	16
Jan 1929	Macdonald	Lab	18	2	4	12	5	—	6	3
Aug 1931	Macdonald	Nat	20	8	10	2	13	6	11	10
Jun 1935	Baldwin	Con	22	9	11	2	14	9	11	10
May 1937	Chamberlain	Con	21	8	13	—	17	8	16	13
May 1945	Churchill	Con	16	6	9	1	14	7	11	9
Aug 1945	Attlee	Lab	20	—	8	12	5	2	10	5
Oct 1951	Churchill	Con	16	5	11	—	14	7	11	9
Apr 1955	Eden	Con	18	5	13	—	18	10	16	14
Jan 1957	Macmillan	Con	18	4	14	—	17	8	16	15
Oct 1963	Home	Con	24	5	19	—	21	11	17	17
Oct 1964	Wilson	Lab	23	1	14	8	8	1	13	11
Jun 1970	Heath	Con	18	4	14	—	15	4	15	15
Mar 1974	Wilson	Lab	21	1	16	4	7	—	16	11
Apr 1976	Callaghan	Lab	22	1	13	7	7	—	15	10
May 1979	Thatcher	Con	22	3	19	—	20	6	18	17

Aristocrats are classed as those whose grandfathers held a hereditary title. The working class members are those whose father had a manual occupation.

Members of the Cabinet

Of the eighteen members of the Tory Cabinet in the summer of 1981, sixteen were the products of an Oxbridge education, the remaining two went to Sandhurst. Trinity College, Cambridge provided six graduates. As for the old school tie, there were six Etonians, two Wykehamists (old boys of Winchester) and one Harrovian. There were a further twelve Old Etonians amongst the thirty-four junior ministers. Eton has provided 40% of *all* the Tory cabinet members since the Second World War. Ministers and their education were as follows:

Margaret Thatcher – Somerville College, Oxford
William Whitelaw – Winchester and Trinity College, Cambridge
Lord Hailsham – Eton and Christchurch College, Oxford
Lord Carrington – Eton and Sandhurst
Sir Geoffrey Howe – Winchester and Trinity College, Cambridge
Sir Keith Joseph – Harrow and Magdalen College, Oxford
John Nott – Trinity College, Cambridge
Lord Soames – Eton and Sandhurst
James Prior – Pembroke College, Cambridge
Sir Ian Gilmour – Eton and Balliol College, Oxford
Roger Edwards – New College, Oxford
Michael Heseltine – Pembroke College, Oxford
Charles Jenkin – Jesus College, Cambridge
Francis Pym – Eton and Magdalen College, Oxford
John Biffen – Jesus College, Cambridge
David Howell – Eton and King's College, Cambridge
Leon Brittan – Trinity College, Cambridge and Yale University
Peter Fowler – Trinity College, Cambridge

Cabinet ministers who have died in office

Butler and Sloman: British Political Facts 1900–79

1916	Lord Kitchener
1925	Marquess Curzon
1930	Lord Thomson
1931	Vernon Hartshorn
1932	Sir Donald Maclean
1936	Sir Godfrey Collins
1940	Sir J. Gilmour
1943	Sir Kingsley Wood
1947	Miss Ellen Wilkinson
1951	Ernest Bevin
1970	Iain Macleod
1977	Anthony Crosland

MPs who have forfeited their seats

Butler and Sloman: British Political Facts 1900–79

After conviction and imprisonment

1903	A. Lynch	(Nat)	Galway
1922	H. Bottomley	(Ind)	Hackney South
1941	Sir P. Latham	(Con)	Scarborough and Whitby
1954	P. Baker	(Con)	South Norfolk
1976	J. Stonehouse	(Lab)	Walsall South

After bankruptcy

1903	P. McHugh	(Nat)	North Leitrim
1909	N. Murphy	(Nat)	South Kilkenny
1928	C. Homan	(Con)	Ashton under Lyne

For holding Government contracts

1904	A. Gibbs	(Con)	City of London	(re-elected)
1904	V. Gibbs	(Con)	St Albans	(defeated)
1912	Sir S. Samuel	(Rad)	Whitechapel	(re-elected)
1925	W. Preston	(Con)	Walsall	(re-elected)

Gave up seat after censure

1931	T. Mordey-Jones	(Lab)	Pontypridd	abuse of travel voucher
1936	Sir A. Butt	(Con)	Balham and Tooting	budget leak
1936	J. Thomas	(Nat Lab)	Derby	budget leak
1947	G. Allighan	(Lab)	Gravesend	breach of privilege
1949	J. Belcher	(Lab)	Sowerby	Lynskey Tribunal
1967	J. Profumo	(Con)	Stratford on Avon	lying to the House
1977	J. Cordle	(Con)	Bournemouth East	Poulson Affair

1916 C. Leach (Lib), from Colne Valley, deprived of seat under Lunacy Act.
1924 J. Aston (Con) from Dover, inadvertently voted before taking the oath –
returned unopposed in subsequent by-election.

Durability of British Prime Ministers, 1900–79

PM	length of service as PM	times in office	age on becoming PM
Marquess of Salisbury	13yrs 9mths	3	55
Herbert Asquith	8yrs 8mths	1	55
Winston Churchill	8yrs 8mths	2	65
Harold Wilson	7yrs 9mths	2	48
Stanley Baldwin	6yrs 10mths	3	56
Ramsay Macdonald	6yrs 9mths	2	58
Harold Macmillan	6yrs 9mths	1	62
Clement Attlee	6yrs 2mths	1	62
David Lloyd George	5yrs 10mths	1	53
Edward Heath	3yrs 8mths	1	53
Arthur Balfour	3yrs 5mths	1	53
James Callaghan	3yrs 1mth	1	64
Neville Chamberlain	2yrs 11mths	1	68
Henry Campbell-Bannerman	2yrs 4mths	1	69
Anthony Eden	1yr 9mths	1	57
Alec Douglas-Home	1yr 0mths	1	60
Andrew Bonar Law	7mths	1	63

Unparliamentary expressions

To finish off all that Parliamentary stuff, and give your eyes a rest from all those facts and figures, here are some rude words.

The Parliamentary 'Bible', Erskine May, suggests that the following expressions should not be used in the House.

calumny	guttersnipe
dishonest	hooligan
duplicity	

MPs are also asked not to call their fellow Members . . .

dogs	rats
cads	stool-pigeons
pharisees	villains
swine	hypocrites
pups	

Nor should they accuse them of . . .

humbug	prevaricating
impertinence	ruffianism
being lousy	being wicked
making a malignant attack	acting in a vicious or vulgar manner

PAYMENTS

Methods of payment used for purchase of goods and services in Great Britain

Inter-bank research organization

| | millions of transactions | |
	1971	1980
Non-cash		
Cheque	450	1 050
Standing order	120	230
Direct debit	40	170
Postal orders	270	125
Credit card	10	130
Credit transfer	40	100
Cash		
All cash payments	over 50 000	over 50 000
Cash payments of 50p and above	10 000	20 000

Credit cards

In mid-1981, credit card holders lined up as follows:

	millions
Barclaycard	5.8
Access	5.1
Trustcard	1.4
American Express	0.6
Diners club	0.25

PHOBIAS

Many of us suffer from one or more of the following fears to some extent. There doesn't appear to be a word for someone who has a phobia about phobias . . .

acrophobia – fear of heights
agoraphobia – fear of open spaces and public places
claustrophobia – fear of confined spaces
entomophobia – fear of insects
erotophobia – fear of sexual intimacy
haphephobia – fear of physical contact
hydrophobia – fear of water
lalophobia – fear of speaking in public
scotophobia – fear of the dark
xenophobia – fear of strangers

PIPES
Pipeman of the Year

Each year since 1964, in an effort to get us to take them seriously, the Pipesmokers' Council has elected a Pipeman of the Year. In 1976 an extra award went to Sir Harold Wilson when he was elected Pipeman of the Decade.

1964	Rupert Davies
1965	Sir Harold Wilson
1966	Andrew Cruickshank
1967	Warren Mitchell
1968	Peter Cushing
1969	Jack Hargreaves
1970	Eric Morecambe
1971	Lord Shinwell
1972	(not awarded)
1973	Frank Muir
1974	Fred Trueman
1975	Sir Campbell Adamson
1976	Sir Harold Wilson (elected Pipeman of the Decade)
1977	Brian Barnes
1978	Magnus Magnusson
1979	J. B. Priestley
1980	Edward Fox
1981	James Galway
1982	Dave Lee Travis

Famous pipesmokers of the past who might have made it, if only there had been a Pipesmokers' Council: Charles Lamb, Sir Isaac Newton, Sir Walter Raleigh, Captain W. E. Johns (author of *Biggles*).

PIRATES

And all of them, says David Ashford, were British to the core.

Henry Morgan
Captain Kidd
Captain John Avery
Bartholemew Roberts
Mary Read
Ann Bonney
Captain Edward England

Howel Davis
Captain Gow
Captain George Lowther
Edward Teach – known as 'Blackbeard'
Captain Spriggs
Captain John Rackham – known as 'Calico Jack'
Charles Vane
Captain Martel
Daniel Benjamin

POISONS
Deadly mother nature

These common plants may look innocent enough and often beautiful, but they all contain poisons which can kill you. If, of course, you eat them. Just looking at them is all right. Go right ahead.

Cherry – leaves and stems
Daphne – berries
Hemlock – the whole plant
Hyacinth – bulbs
Laburnum – seeds and flowers
Larkspur – seeds
Nightshade – whole plant
Oleander – leaves and branches
Rhododendron – whole plant
Rhubarb – leaves
Yew – berries and foliage

POLLUTION
Oil spills requiring clean-ups in 1980
Advisory Committee on Oil Pollution of the Sea

Coastal divisions

Essex and Kent	49
Eastern Scotland	28
Southern England	25
Bristol Channel and South Wales	25
Eastern England	9
North Eastern England	7
Cornwall	7
Orkney and Shetland Isles	7
North Sea offshore oilfields	7
Sussex	6
Lancashire and Western districts	6
Western Scotland	5
Total	181

There was also a significant number of unreported spillages. Local authorities have the responsibility for cleaning coastlines and estuaries and the collective cost in 1979 was £69 000. In 1980 it was £113 000.

POPULATION
Population at each census, 1951–81
Census 81: Preliminary report, England and Wales

	thousands			
England	*1951*	*1961*	*1971*	*1981*
Males	19 746	21 012	22 356	22 471
Females	21 414	22 448	23 663	23 750
All persons	41 159	43 461	46 018	46 221

Great Britain	1951	1961	1971	1981
Males	23 450	24 787	26 198	26 286
Females	25 404	26 497	27 781	27 842
All persons	48 854	51 284	53 979	54 129

Population growth in the seventies was much less than in the previous two decades. The percentage increase was 0.3, the smallest ever since censuses began in 1801.

The provisional count for the UK in 1981 shows 1058 females for every 1000 males.

Population density: International comparison

UN Demographic Year Book 1977

	number of people per square km 1970		number of people per square km 1970
Netherlands	415	Spain	74
Belgium	319	Greece	73
Japan	314	Turkey	58
West Germany	247	Irish Republic	49
UK	229	USA	24
India	202	Sweden	18
Italy	189	Brazil	14
Luxembourg	133	USSR	12
Denmark	119	New Zealand	12
Portugal	108	Australia	2
China	100	Canada	2
France	98		

World population is estimated to have grown by 22% since 1970.

POSTCARDS
National Portrait Gallery's most popular postcard reproductions, 1981

In alphabetical order:

The Brontë Sisters
Elizabeth I
Henry VIII
Lady Jane Grey
T. E. Lawrence
The Prince and Princess of Wales
Queen Victoria
Richard III
Virginia Woolf

In 1981 the Gallery had its third highest attendance ever – 529 608.

Most popular postcard themes with UK collectors

1	Typographical	6	Military
2	Glamour	7	Political
3	Artists	8	Royalty
4	Advertising	9	Ships
5	Humour	10	Costumes

QUIZ LIST

Do you ever listen to those dopey competitions they always seem to have on those dopey radio programmes? It's usually a half-witted housewife on the telephone, saying yes, yes, she knows the tune, but she just can't remember the name. If it's not a housewife, then it's probably Bob Woodhead.

He wrote to us, boasting that he is the country's radio quiz champion, having won over 50 competitions in the last two years, most of them about pop music. He is 26 and lives in South Mundham, Chichester. He has a law degree but was unemployed at the time. It was to give himself something to do that he started entering all these radio contests. To give himself even more to do he has compiled the following lists.

My worst prizes

1   A wall scroll from BBC Radio One giving me a 'free pardon' for my 'confession'.
2   A bottle of Pomagne from my local radio station. They refused to send it and it would have cost me twice as much to go and collect it.
3   A pocket calculator that changes its mind, even with fresh batteries.
4   A Biro that writes purple. Yuck.
5   A Peter Powell photo and badge.
6   An LP by the punk rock group The Vibrators.

My best prizes

1   Ten LP records of my choice (worth £50). I won this prize three times, but it took a solicitor's letter to get me the third batch, after which the station decided the only way to stop me winning was to stop the competition.
2   Capital Radio 'Winner' sweatshirt (worth £7). Again I won this prize three times, and again it led to them stopping the competition.
3   £15 in cash, for lasting the whole week on a pop quiz. After three months the local station had forgotten me, and I won it again!
4   Five Top 30 LPs (numbers of my choice) and a sunstrip, on BBC Radio Two's *Music Game*.
5   Three LP record tokens and a £5 book, for answering detailed questions on The Beatles on BBC Radio One.

My easiest questions

1 The song 'Sorrow' was a hit in 1966 for a group from Liverpool who used to be called the Merseybeats. What was their new name?
  Answer: The Merseys.
2 Who had a hit in 1965 with 'It's good news week'?
  Answer: Hedgehoppers Anonymous.
  This question came up for me twice in a matter of weeks, on two different radio stations.
3 Name ten First Division Football grounds in 60 seconds.
  Well, for a football fanatic like me . . . it took 20 seconds. I won't bother to put the answer.
4 Where and when was the last time The Beatles all played together live?
  Answer: 30 January 1969 – on top of the 'Apple' building in Savile Row, London. I was so quick off the mark that the DJ then asked me for the colour of their socks.
5 Which Roman city in Italy got buried in volcanic ash, with a clue that you should think of the local football team?
  Answer: Pompeii (this was on the Portsmouth local station – hence the 'Pompey' football team).

My hardest questions

1 What month and in what year was Benny Hill's 'Ernie' number 1?
  Answer: It was number 1 in December 1971 and January 1972 for four weeks. I had to go for one of them, and went for January. Needless to say their answer was December!
2 Who did Cassius Clay fight in Madison Square Garden in March 1963?
  Answer: Doug Jones (who's he?).
3 I was given five snatches of old pop songs, lasting half-a-second each (total time about three seconds), and had to identify them to win £50 worth of LP records of my choice.
4 Which Beatle songs did Truth and The Silkie take into the charts?
  Answer: 'Girl' and 'You've Got to Hide Your Love Away', both very minor hits in the mid-60s.

5   Which rock band did Vincent Crane play in?
    Answer: Atomic Rooster. I made a sheer guess, out of
    hundreds of groups, and got it right, or perhaps I sub-
    consciously knew.

QUOTES

Of all the professions, about the only one held in lower esteem
than journalism is politics. Both journalists and politicians are
apt to talk nonsense, but only politicians can impose taxes as
well.

Here are ten examples of choice remarks made by
politicians and journalists. Thanks to Don Atyeo and
Jonathon Green, whose book *Don't Quote Me* (Hamlyn
Paperbacks) was of invaluable assistance.

'I wish I hadn't said that'

1   **Leon Trotsky** (1925) – 'England is ripe for revolution.'
2   **Lord Beaverbrook** (1932) – 'Churchill? He's a busted
    flush!'
3   **Sir Oswald Mosley** (1938) – 'We (the Black Shirts) shall
    reach the helm in five years.'
4   **The Daily Express** (1938) – 'The Daily Express Declares
    That Britain Will Not Be Involved In A European War
    This Year Or Next Year Either.'
5   **Neville Chamberlain** (1938) – 'I believe it is peace for our
    time.'
6   **Lord Beaverbrook** (1945), speaking of the forthcoming
    General Election – 'I am convinced that Churchill will
    carry his party to victory.' Churchill lost.
7   **John Profumo** (1963) – 'There was no impropriety what-
    soever in my relationship with Christine Keeler.'
8   **Harold Wilson** (1966) – 'Britain is swinging, but swinging
    into action, not decay.'
9   **Margaret Thatcher** (1969) – 'No woman in my time will
    be Prime Minister or Chancellor or Foreign Secretary –
    not the top jobs. Anyway, I wouldn't want to be Prime
    Minister; you have to give yourself 100%.'

10 **Shirley Williams** (1980) – 'I am not interested in a third party. I do not believe that it has any future.'

Quotes of 1981

1 'My wife isn't speaking to me.' – *The Barnsley man who fogot to send off the pools coupon that would have won his wife £750 000*

2 'Academic staff rather like coming to conclusions, but they don't like making decisions at all.' – *Lord Annan*

3 'We are not just a minor party; we are a unique experience.' – *David Owen*

4 'I feel positively delighted and frankly amazed that Diana is prepared to take me on.' – *Prince Charles*

5 'A man who is old enough to die for his country is old enough to decide who to sleep with.' – *Joint Council for Gay Teenagers*

6 'Elections are so healing.' – *Tony Benn*

7 'People can say what they want in the Labour Party.' – *Michael Foot*

8 'The best way to pay tribute to the people who died in the First and Second World Wars is to make sure that there isn't a Third.' – *Michael Foot*

9 'This band has no politics; we're just pissed off.' – *Hoxteth Tom, bassist for the 'Oi' band, the 4-Skins*

10 'Mai Tai Finn is one of the students in the programme and was in the centre of the photograph. We incorrectly listed her name as one of the items on the menu.' – *Community Life Magazine*

RACING
First past the post

Almost every racing year throws up one horse whose winnings, even before anyone has collected on their bets, puts them a class above their rivals. These are horses that have dominated a single year since the early 1970s, when prize money began to leap in value:

winnings	horse	age	year
£394 646	Shergar	3	1981
£310 539	Troy	3	1979
£236 332	Ela-Mana-Mou	3	1980
£201 184	The Minstrel	3	1977
£188 375	Grundy	3	1975
£166 389	Wollow	3	1976
£159 681	Nijinsky	3	1970
£151 213	Brigadier Gerard	4	1972
£136 012	Ile de Bourbon	3	1978
£121 913	Mill Reef	3	1971
£120 771	Dahlia	4	1974

But hang on: in 1973 Dahlia, as a three-year-old, was also top money winner in Britain, with a 'modest' total of £79 230. This double achievement is unequalled since the war. So there.

The champions

All the riders this century who have earned the title of Champion Jockey on more than one occasion:

26 times	Gordon Richards	1925–53
10	Lester Piggott	1960–81
10	Steve Donoghue	1914–23 (one shared)
5	Doug Smith	1954–59
4	Frank Wootton	1909–12
	Scobie Breasley	1957–63
	Willie Carson	1972–80
	Pat Eddery	1974–77
3	Otto Madden	1901–04
2	Billy Higgs	1906, 1907
	Charlie Elliott	1923, 1924 (one shared)

The hard men

Riding National Hunt races is a hard job; riding to win is harder; riding more winners than anyone else time and time again is hardest of all; the following heroes have all won the jockeys' championship at least twice this century:

7 times	Gerry Wilson	1932/33–1940/41
6	Tich Mason	1901–07
5	Fred Rees	1920–1926/27
	Billy Stott	1927/28–1931/32
	Tim Molony	1948/49–1954/55
4	Fred Winter	1952/53–1957/58
	Josh Gifford	1962/63–1967/68
	Fred Rimell	1938/39–1945/46 (one shared)
3	Ernie Piggott	1910–1915
	Stan Mellor	1959/60–1961/62
	John Francome	1975/76–1980/81
	Terry Biddlecombe	1964/65–1968/69 (one shared)
	Bob Davies	1968/69–1971/72 (one shared)
2	Jack Anthony	1914, 1922
	Ron Barry	1972/73, 1973/74
	Tommy Stack	1974/75, 1976/77
	Jonjo O'Neill	1977/78, 1979/80

RADIO
Top BBC radio programmes, 1980–81

	programme	estimated audience	1979 placing
1	*Top 40* (Sunday, Radio 1)	7 100 000	(1)
2	Noel Edmonds (Sunday, Radio 1)	4 200 000	(4)
3	Terry Wogan (Weekdays, Radio 2)	3 600 000	(2)
4	*Junior Choice* (Saturday, Radio 1)	3 100 000	(3)
5	Jimmy Savile's *Old Record Club* (Sunday, Radio 1)	2 700 000	(—)
6	Jimmy Young (Weekdays, Radio 2)	2 500 000	(5)

	7	8 a.m. *News* (Weekdays, Radio 4)	2 300 000	(6)
	8	Pete Murray (Sunday, Radio 2)	1 800 000	(—)
	9	*Today* (Weekdays, Radio 4)	1 600 000	(7=)
	10	Pete Murray (Saturday, Radio 2)	1 500 000	(—)

In 1979, Radio 4's 1.00 p.m. *News* tied for seventh place with the *Today* programme. Last year it dropped out of the Top Ten together with *Any Questions* and *Start the Week* (respectively ninth and tenth in 1979). Newcomers to the list are Jimmy Savile and Pete Murray.

Radio listening per head per week

hours and minutes per head per week

	national	independent local radio	BBC local radio	Luxembourg
1976	6 55	1 14	0 35	0 05
1978	6 49	1 21	0 38	0 04
1979	7 06	1 21	0 37	0 03
1980	7 12	1 27	0 38	0 03

RECORDS
Paul McCartney's favourite records

On the occasion of the fortieth anniversary of Roy Plomley's radio show *Desert Island Discs*, Paul McCartney – the world's most successful composer of popular music – was asked to name the eight records he would take with him to the island. His choice was:

1 *Heartbreak Hotel* – Elvis Presley
2 *Sweet Little Sixteen* – Chuck Berry
3 *The Courtly Dance* from *Gloriana* – played by Julian Bream
4 *Be-Bop-A-Lula* – Gene Vincent
5 *Beautiful Boy* – John Lennon
6 *Searching* – The Coasters
7 *Tutti-Frutti* – Little Richard
8 *Walking in the Park With Eloise* – written by his father, James McCartney

REPRODUCTIONS
Best-selling Athena reproductions

1 *Jasper* by Gertrude Halsband
2 *Mandolin* by Ha Van Vuong
3 *Evening Tide* by Jim Spencer
4 *Willow's Edge* by Colin Paynton
5 *Four Seasons* by Chris Dodds
6 *Frosty Stile* by Colin Paynton
7 *Beach Scene* by Mick Durrant
8 *Swans Reflecting Elephants* by Salvador Dali
9 *Station Approach* by L. S. Lowry
10 *Bois Gibault* by Ha Van Huong

Their best-selling reproductions of masterpieces are Monet's *Poppies* and Picasso's *Blue Model*. The best-selling poster is *Tennis Girl*.

ROLLS ROYCE

At last, a list where Britain is top of the league, in quantity as well as quality.

Number of Rolls Royce cars bought in 1981

UK	1 218
USA	1 158
France	119
Saudi Arabia	107
Australia	84
Switzerland	73
West Germany	68
Bahrain*	59
Canada	58
Kuwait	54
Italy	51
Hong Kong	50

* including associated states.

ROYALTY

Amounts payable from central funds under the Civil Lists Act to members of the Royal Family in the calendar year 1981.

Royalties

	£
The Queen	3 260 200
The Queen Mother	286 000
Duke of Edinburgh	160 000
Duke of Kent	106 000
Princess Alexandra	101 000
Princess Anne	100 000
Princess Margaret	98 000
Duke of Gloucester	78 000
Duchess of Gloucester	40 000

Prince Andrew and Prince Edward: £20 000 from the time they reach the age of 18 until they marry. This increases to £50 000 on their marriage.

There is no specific provision for the Prince of Wales – but he receives the revenue of the Duchy of Cornwall.

The greater part of the money is required to meet official expenses.

Royal Duties

So what did we get for all that money? A loyal reader of *The Times*, Mr T. C. M. O'Donovan, carried out a survey of the duties performed by the Royal Family during 1981, as reported in *The Times* Court Circular.

	1	2	3	4	5
The Queen	102	69	1	108	5
Duke of Edinburgh	150	106	37	9	11
The Queen Mother	49	28	1	12	8
Prince of Wales	118	44	16	30	1
Princess Anne	50	21	2	7	4
Princess Margaret	67	22	3	4	5

	1	2	3	4	5
Prince Alice, Duchess of Gloucester	36	19	5	7	1
Duke of Gloucester	69	31	10	3	5
Duchess of Gloucester	57	19	2	—	2
Duke of Kent	79	21	11	9	7
Duchess of Kent	64	18	4	2	—
Princess Alexandra	79	29	3	7	2

1 Official visits, opening ceremonies and other appearances including charity galas and premieres.
2 Receptions, lunches, dinners and banquets.
3 Meetings presided over and attended.
4 Audiences given.
5 Overseas tours and visits. (These involve many public appearances which are not recorded.)

In addition, The Queen held 29 investitures and received 85 Ambassadors and High Commissioners in audience, the Queen Mother seven, Princess Anne four and Princess Margaret 11. The Queen also presided over 13 meetings of the Privy Council, and gave weekly audiences to the Prime Minister.

RUGBY
Stalwart Lions

Great Britain and Ireland join forces to play Rugby Union only on tours abroad. The following players lead the honours board in representing the British Isles – the Lions – in international matches:

17 times	W. J. McBride	Ireland
13	R. E. G. Jeeps	England
12	C. M. H. Gibson	Ireland
10	G. O. Edwards	Wales
	J. J. F. O'Reilly	Ireland
	R. H. Williams	Wales

9 times	A. R. Irvine	Scotland
8	D. I. E. Bebb	Wales
	P. Bennett	Wales
	G. L. Brown	Scotland
	M. J. Campbell-Lamerton	Scotland
	T. M. Davies	Wales
	I. R. McGeechan	Scotland
	I. McLauchlan	Scotland
	B. V. Meredith	Wales
	S. Millar	Ireland
	N. A. A. Murphy	Ireland
	A. E. I. Pask	Wales
	G. Price	Wales
	J. W. Telfer	Scotland
	J. P. R. Williams	Wales

Long-serving internationals

Rugby players tend not to last as long as their soccer-playing counterparts – and any international player who notches up fifty appearances for his country has done sterling service. The following list includes all international appearances, including Tests for the British Isles on representative tours abroad.

81 caps	Mike Gibson	Ireland
80	Willie John McBride	Ireland
63	Gareth Edwards	Wales
63	J. P. R. Williams	Wales
59	Tom Kiernan	Ireland
56*	Fergus Slattery	Ireland
55	Colin Meads	New Zealand
53*	Andy Irvine	Scotland
52	Jack Kyle	Ireland
52	Roland Bertranne	France
51	Gerald Davies	Wales

51 caps	Ian McLauchlan	Scotland
50	Benoit Dauga	France
50	Sandy Carmichael	Scotland

* Up to 31 December 1981; Slattery and Irvine are both still playing rugby at international level.

The most capped Englishman is John Pullin, with a total of 49.

SAINTLY SAYINGS

St Swithin isn't the only saint said to be responsible for predicting the weather. Countrymen have for centuries worked out their own forecasting system according to many other saints. Well, someone has to take the blame. There are hundreds of these sayings. Here is one for each month.

JANUARY
25th *Conversion of St Paul*
If it be a fair day, it will be a pleasant year. If it be windy, there will be wars; if it be cloudy, it foreshadows the plague.

FEBRUARY
2nd *Purification of the Blessed Virgin Mary (Candlemas)*
If Candlemas-day be fair and bright,
Winter will have another flight:
But if it be dark with clouds and rain,
Winter is gone and won't come again.
If Candlemas day be fine and clear,
Corn and fruit will then be dear.
If the wind's in the east on Candlemas Day
It's sure to stay to the second of May.

MARCH
1st *St David's Day*
Upon St David's Day, put oats and barley in the clay.

149

APRIL
6th *Old Lady Day*
On Lady-Day the latter
The cold comes over the water.

MAY
12th *St Pancras*
There is a belief on the continent that very cold weather, a second winter, may be expected in the middle of May.

JUNE
15th *St Vitus*
If St Vitus's day be rainy weather
It will rain for thirty days together.

JULY
15th *St Swithin*
If St Swithin weeps the proverb says,
The weather will be foul for forty days.

AUGUST
10th *St Laurence*
If it rain on St Laurence, it is rather late but still in time.

SEPTEMBER
29th *St Michael*
If Michaelmas day be fine, the sun will shine much in the winter, though the wind at north-east will frequently reign long and be sharp and nipping.

OCTOBER:
18th *St Luke*
At St Luke's day kill your pigs and bung up your barrels.
Up to St Luke's day put your hands where you like; after it keep them in your pockets.

NOVEMBER:
1st *All Saints*
On All Saints day, cut off some bark from a beech tree, and

after that, a chip or a piece of wood; if it be dry, then the ensuing winter will be dry, but pretty warm and temperate, if moist, a wet winter.

DECEMBER:
28th   *Innocents' Day*
If it be lowering or wet on Innocents' Day, it threatens scarcity and mortality among the weaker sort of young people: but if the day be very fair, it promises plenty.

SALES
Sotheby's of London's assorted world records, 1981

1   *World record for a Chinese work of art*
Ming blue-and-white jar of the Xuande Period
(1426–35)   £720 000

2   *World record for a Western illuminated manuscript*
The Ottobeuren Gradual and Sacramentary
written and illuminated at the Benedictine
Abbey of Ottobeuren, c. 1194   £700 000

3   *World record for any tapestry*
Medieval tapestry frieze made in northern
Switzerland (1468–76)   £550 000

4   *World record for Wedgwood porcelain*
'Sneyd' Wedgwood copy of the Portland Vase,
c. 1797   £27 000

5   *World record for a philatelic envelope from the
Far East*
The unique item showing the cancellation number
allotted by the British Post Office to Hiogo –
17 March, 1879   £46 000

6   *World record for a Chiparus figure*
Bronze and ivory figure seated in the Lotus
position – 1920s   £24 000

7   *World record for a silver spoon*
A rare Edward IV slip-top spoon marked with an
annulet over a chevron, *c.* 1465   £9 200
8   *World record for a single bottle of twentieth-century*
vintage wine
One Imperial of Chateau Mouton Rothschild
1929   £4 400
9   *World record for a Greek icon*
Seventeenth-century Cretan icon representing
the Tree of Jesse   £42 000
10 *World record for a Julia Margaret Cameron*
photograph
Profile portrait of Virginia Woolf's mother –
April 1867   £5 500
11 *World record for a golf ball*
Feathery ball by William Gourley and another
by T. Morri   each £800
12 *World record for any celluloid*
The Three Caballeros, an original Walt Disney
celluloid, signed 'To Art Doyle, Best Wishes
Walt Disney'   £1 100
13 *World record for a costume design*
Costume design for the ballet *Le Dieu Bleu* by
Leon Bakst – 1911   £15 500

Phillips' assorted sales records, 1981

Let's now go round the corner from Bond Street and see how
Phillips auctions did in 1981.

Their interesting items sold in 1981 included a 'pile of
firewood' and a sandwich. There were also some world
records in price and in size – both large and small:

1 *'Mirror, mirror on the wall . . .'*
A West Country man who 'does up mirrors for a hobby' was
removing the glass from a Victorian overmantle mirror when
he discovered a small painting which had been used as a

backing panel. The picture was of the English School *c*. 1800 and it fetched £450 at the Bath saleroom.

2 *Jumbo ivories*

To launch regular piano sales, Phillips auctioned the world's largest piano – a white-painted grand weighing 1¼ tons made in 1935 to commemorate the Silver Jubilee of King George V and Queen Mary. The monster unfortunately turned out to be a 'white elephant' and failed to sell.

3 *War games*

The largest ever collection of lead soldiers and figures, numbering almost 17 000 items made by Britains and collected by L. W. Richards, was sold by Phillips in 1981 for a record £69 000. Highlights included a 3in-high Camel Corps Trooper (costing twopence in 1910!) which made £260 and became the world's most expensive toy soldier. A civilian motorcycle and sidecar model reached a staggering £960.

4 *Royal supports*

A pair of bookends made from the epaulettes of one of King George V's uniforms was sold at Phillips for £150 in December.

5 *A model customer?*

One day, the landlord of the Old Greyhound pub at Caterham, Surrey, had to refuse one of his regulars any further credit at the bar. The customer, a butcher by trade, went away and returned a few weeks later with an elaborate model of a Victorian butcher's shop complete with joints of meat and a shop cat. The publican was so pleased with the gift that he wiped the slate clean. The model fetched £720.

6 *Money to burn?*

What looked just like a pile of firewood made £500 at a sale of musical instruments. The eight pieces of seasoned maple, each measuring 16 inches by 9 inches, were ideal for the construction of violin-backs.

7 *Pot of gold*

In 1962, retired builder Mr George Cottrell stuck together some 'couple of dozen pieces of coloured pot' which he had found in the yard of a smallholding he had just bought. He filled up a gap in the lip of the 'pot' with cement and planted flowers in it. Then in 1975 he dug up the missing piece in his vegetable patch. When a dealer came to look at some furniture Mr Cottrell wanted to sell in 1981, he immediately recognized the 'Chinese pot' as a Ming jar of the Chia Ching period, more than four hundred years old. The jar was the centre of attention at Phillips in December 1981 when it sold for £16 000.

8   *A lot of nonsense*

A bag of Smokey Bacon Crisps and a cheese and pickle sandwich became collectors' items under the hammer at Phillips on 1 April 1981. 'Lot 53' sold for £15 and the proceeds were donated to charity.

SCHOOLCHILDREN
Pupils in secondary education in England
Department of Education and Science

	1971 %	1980 %
Middle deemed secondary	1.9	6.9
Modern	38.0	6.8
Grammar	18.4	3.7
Technical	1.3	0.3
Comprehensive	34.4	81.4
Other	6.0	1.0
Total pupils (in thousands)	2 953	3 866

SCOUTS
Notable former Scouts

A selection of well-known personalities who are pleased to acknowledge their one-time membership of the Scout Movement.

Peter Adamson (Coronation Street)
David Attenborough
Richard Attenborough
Richard Baker
Tony Benn MP
Michael Barrett
Frank Bough
Bernard Bresslaw
Roy Castle
Christopher Chataway
Bishop of Chelmsford
Lewis Collins
Tommy Cooper
Kenneth Cope
Tony Curtis
Peter Cushing
Horace Cutler
Les Dawson
Jim Davidson
Ken Dodd
Val Doonican
Dick Emery
Georgie Fame
Cary Grant
Deryck Guyler
Rolf Harris
Ron Hayward (Secretary, Labour Party)
James Hayter
Eric Heffer MP
Frankie Howard
Sir Geoffrey Howe MP

Michael Hurll
Gordon Jackson
Lionel Jeffries
Brian Johnson
Roy Kinnear
Danny La Rue
Sammy Lee
Jimmy Logan
Malcolm Macdonald
Harold Macmillan
Gerry Marsden
James Mason
Roy Mason MP
Paul McCartney
James McKechnie
Bob Monkhouse
Stirling Moss
Derek Nimmo
Denis Norden
Tom O'Connor
Dr David Owen
Jack Parnell
Gordon Pirie
Brian Rix
William Rushton
Norman Rossington
Doug Scott
Tommy Trinder
Wynford Vaughan-Thomas
Edward Woodward
Sir Harold Wilson
Norman Wisdom

SELF-SUFFICIENCY
Percentage of UK self-sufficiency in selected products, 1980–81
Eurostat

	%		%
Crops:		cheese	68
wheat	76	butter	42
rye	73	beef	76
barley	110	veal	136
oats	95	pork	63
Total grain	78	poultry	100
		meat	73
potatoes	96	oil/fats	10
sugar	44		
vegetables	79		
fresh fruit	34		

SEXUALLY-TRANSMITTED DISEASES
New patients seen at hospital clinics, 1980
DHSS

cases (in all stages) dealt with for the first time at any centre		*thousands*
Gonorrhoea	*male*	38
	female	23
Non-specific genital infection	*male*	96
	female	29
Other conditions requiring treatment	*male*	88
	female	105

Other conditions not requiring treatment	*male*	74
	female	43
Syphilis	*male*	3
	female	1
Total	*male*	299
	female	201
Persons under 20 dealt with for syphilis or gonorrhoea	*male*	5
	female	7

Sexually-transmitted diseases were on the increase between 1971 and 1980 – in males by almost half; in females by two thirds. The figures are only a guide as they relate only to patients in contact with the NHS.

SHOPS
No longer serving

Some famous shops which have disappeared – victims of closure and takeover or re-organization.

Bon Marché
Bourne & Hollingsworth
Debenham and Freebody
Derry and Toms
Fifty Shilling Tailors
Gamages
Gorringes
Marshall and Snelgrove
Pontings
Swan and Edgar
Whiteley's

SMOKING
Cigarette-smoking habits by age and sex
General Household Survey

	1972 %	1980 %
Men		
Never or only occasionally smoked	25	30
Ex-regular smokers	23	28
Current smokers	52	42
Women		
Never or only occasionally smoked	49	49
Ex-regular smokers	10	14
Current smokers	41	37

Cigarette smoking has continued to decline amongst men but not amongst women. Cigarette smoking is much higher in the manual than non-manual occupation groups. And is this a puff for the cigarette industry? Discuss.

SNOOKER

Only once has the world professional snooker title left the United Kingdom. These are the winners since the championship's inception in 1927:

World Snooker Champions

1927–40	Joe Davis (England)
1941–45	*no competition*
1946	Joe Davis (England)
1947	Walter Donaldson (Scotland)
1948–49	Fred Davis (England)
1950	Walter Donaldson (Scotland)

1951–56	Fred Davis (England)
1957	John Pulman (England)
1958–63	*no competition*
1964–68	John Pulman (England)
1969	John Spencer (England)
1970	Ray Reardon (Wales)
1971	John Spencer (England)
1972	Alex Higgins (Northern Ireland)
1973–76	Ray Reardon (Wales)
1977	John Spencer (England)
1978	Ray Reardon (Wales)
1979	Terry Griffiths (Wales)
1980	Cliff Thorburn (Canada)
1981	Steve Davis (England)
1982	Alex Higgins (Northern Ireland)

STAMPS

Stamp collecting is the world's most popular collecting hobby. (Of all the world's hobbies, it is generally ranked as number two after photography.) There are four million serious stamp collectors in Britain.

These 1982 lists have been provided by Stanley Gibbons, London, the largest international stamp dealers in the world.

The top ten British stamps

approximate values, 1982

1	1902–04 King Edward VII 6d, dull purple, Inland Revenue overprint	£50 000 unused £30 000 used
2	1864–79 Queen Victoria 1d, red, plate 77	£35 000 unused £18 000 used
3	1882 Queen Victoria £1, brown-lilac, (watermark large anchor)	£30 000 unused £2 000 used

4	1878 Queen Victoria £1, brown-lilac, (watermark Maltese cross)	£25 000 unused £1 300 used
5	1902–04 King Edward VII 1/-, green-red, Board of Education overprint	£23 000 unused £10 000 used
6	1883 Queen Victoria 10/-, grey (watermark large anchor)	£22 000 unused £1 100 used
7	1878 Queen Victoria 10/-, grey (watermark Maltese Cross)	£20 000 unused £900 used
8	1885 Queen Victoria £1, brown-lilac, Inland Revenue overprint (watermark three crowns)	£18 000 unused £3 000 used
9	1902 King Edward VII 10/-, blue, Inland Revenue overprint	£17 000 unused £9 500 used
10	1890 Queen Victoria £1, brown-lilac, Inland Revenue overprint (watermark three orbs)	£15 000 unused £2 750 used
	1902 King Edward VII £1, green, Inland Revenue overprint	£15 000 unused £3 250 used

Notice that a Penny Black, Britain's best known stamp, is not in the list. Although it was the first postage stamp in the world in 1840, 69 million were printed. A Penny Black in top condition is worth about £2500.

Countries most collected by stamp collectors living in UK

1 Great Britain
2 New Zealand
3 Australia
4 Canada
5 USA

6 Hong Kong
7 Falkland Islands
8 Vatican
9 Israel
10 Ireland

Most popular stamp themes

Apart from collecting countries, many collectors also collect stamps on a theme, a speciality which is growing all the time.

1 Music
2 Flowers
3 Animals
4 Chess
5 Art
6 Boy scouts
7 Sports
8 Heraldry/Uniforms
9 Health/Medicine
10 Birds

Unusual stamp themes

1 Windmills
2 Running camels
3 Sugar cane
4 Waterfalls
5 Mining
6 Fossils
7 Dictators
8 Stamps on stamps
9 Bananas
10 Weapons

Top ten world stamps, 1982

(approximate prices)

		price (£)	condition
1	British Guiana 1 cent black on magenta of 1856	425 000	unused
2	Mauritius 'Post Office' 1d red of 1847	375 000 140 000	unused used
3	Mauritius 'Post Office' 2d blue of 1847	240 000 140 000	unused used
4	Bermuda red 'Penny Perot' 1848–61	100 000	used
5	Hawaii 2 cents blue of 1851	60 000 30 000	unused used
6	British Guiana 2 cents rose 'Cotton Reel' 1851	55 000	used
7	Great Britain 1902 6d purple 'IR OFFICIAL'	50 000 25 000	unused used
8	Ceylon 4d dull rose of 1857	50 000 4 500	unused used
9	Canada 12d black of 1851	42 000 38 000	unused used
10	Great Britain 1864–79 Queen Victoria 1d red plate 77	35 000 18 000	unused used

STRIPS
The ten best British newspaper strip cartoons

At least according to George Perry (yes, him again), author of *The Penguin Book of Comics*.

1 Flook (*Daily Mail*)
2 Bristow (*The Standard*)
3 Andy Capp (*Daily Mirror*)
4 Jane (*Daily Mirror*)
5 Fred Basset (*Daily Mail*)
6 Rupert (*Daily Express*)
7 Carol Day (*Daily Mail*)
8 Pop (*Daily Sketch*)
9 Jeff Hawke (*Daily Express*)
10 Modesty Blaise (*The Standard*)

SUICIDES
Seven suicide victims

		mode of suicide	year
1	Thomas Chatterton	arsenic poisoning	1770
2	Virginia Woolf	drowning	1941
3	Lady Isobel Barnett	electrocution	1980
4	Clive of India	stabbing	1774
5	Tony Hancock	overdose	1968
6	Captain L. E. G. Oates	walking into blizzard	1912
7	Lord Castlereagh	cut throat	1822

SWIMMING
Olympians triumphant

In a sport dominated for so much of its recent history by the USA, Australia and, in the modern era, Eastern Europe,

Great Britain has had to struggle hard for Olympic medals of any colour (though only in 1936 and 1972 did Britain fail to return with at least one medal). This is the roll call of Britain's Olympic gold medal winners:

MEN

1908	Henry Taylor	400 metres freestyle
	Henry Taylor	1500 metres freestyle
	Fred Holman	200 metres breaststroke
	4 × 200 metres relay team (John Darbyshire, Paul Radmilovic, William Foster, Henry Taylor)	
1912	Water Polo team	
1920	Water Polo team	
1976	David Wilkie	200 metres breaststroke
1980	Duncan Goodhew	100 metres breaststroke

WOMEN

1912	4 × 100 metres freestyle relay team (Bella Moore, Jennie Fletcher, Annie Spiers, Irene Steer)	
1924	Lucy Morton	200 metres breaststroke
1956	Judy Grinham	100 metres backstroke
1960	Anita Lonsbrough	200 metres breaststroke

TEETH

Percentage of people with no natural teeth, England and Wales

Office of Population Censuses and Surveys

age	1968	1978
16–24	1	—
25–34	7	3
35–44	22	12
45–54	41	29

164

age	1968	1978
55–64	64	48
65–74	79	74
75 and over	88	87

The greatest improvement is in the middle age group. In the North, 33% had no natural teeth. In London and the South-east, 21%. Women are more likely to lose teeth than men: in 1978, 32% of women and 24% of men had no natural teeth.

TELEPHONES
The numbers game

British Telecom

*Total number of telephones, 1981	27 870 000
*Number of telephones per 1000 population	498
Total number of calls dialled	20 292 000 000
Total number of inland calls	20 175 000 000
Total number of international calls	116 599 000
Percentage of all calls dialled direct	96%
*Annual calling rate (per instrument):	
Local	616.8
Trunk	122.2
International	4.3
Number of call boxes	76 985
Average annual income per call box	£1 104.12

*Figures refer to individual instruments and not to exchange connections. One exchange connection may have several instruments all with the same number.

Telephone calls to recorded information services, 1980-81

British Telecom

	millions
Speaking clock	404.1
Dial a disc	102.5
Cricket	30.5
Weather	26.3
Financial Times index	3.8
Recipe	2.5
Motoring	1.2
Other recorded services:	
racing, tennis, gardening, etc	44.8
Total calls to recorded information services	615.7

Calls have increased by 68% since 1970–71.

Former names of London telephone exchanges

When all-figure Exchange codes were introduced in 1966, London lost some of its most picturesque names. Here are some of the most attractive together with their new numbers:

Acorn   01-992
Anvil   01-593
Bluebell   01-656
Cherrywood   01-540
Clocktower   01-552
Coppermill   01-520
Diligence   01-903
Dreadnought   01-371
Duke   01-931
Enterprise   01-368

Floral   01-878
Galleon   01-330
Hop   01-407
Ivanhoe   01-505
Juniper   01-586
Laburnum   01-360
Mulberry   01-889
Noble   01-602
Spartan   01-249
Trojan   01-870

Odd telephone exchanges

STD Codebook

London might have lost those nice names, but in the UK as a whole there are still many places worth ringing, if only to find out where they are.

Back
Blubberhouses
Bwlch
Drumbo
Esh Winning
Eye
Fence Houses
Haugh-of-Urr
Knockin
Lower Peover
Mid Yell
Piddletrenthide
Prickwillow
Ripe
Six Mile Bottom
Wideopen
Ynysybwl

TELEVISION

Top television programmes, 1981

Jictar/BBC to 31 July, BARB from 1 August

From 1 August 1981, the calculation and publication of comparative viewing figures was taken over by the Broadcasters' Audience Research Board Ltd – BARB. Until that date the information had been compiled separately by Jictar and the BBC Audience Research Unit. Consquently the following figures have been obtained by a combination of different sampling methods. Ian Marter did all the work. Phew.

TOP FIVE FOR 1981 (excluding movies)

		highest audience (millions)
1	*Coronation Street* (Granada)	20.80
2	*The Benny Hill Show* (Thames)	20.00
3	*This Is Your Life* (Thames)	19.70
4	*To the Manor Born* (BBC)	17.75
5	*Magnum* (ITV)	17.60

Of these:
Coronation Street appeared in the monthly Top Five 28 times
The Benny Hill Show   6
This Is Your Life   3
To The Manor Born   3
Magnum   1

Other programmes reaching the monthly Top Five placings were:
A Town Like Alice (BBC)   twice
Hart To Hart (BBC)
Are You Being Served? (BBC)
Bergerac (BBC)
ITN News (ITN)
Morecambe and Wise (Thames)

Nine O'Clock News (BBC)
Shelley (Thames)
Sorry (BBC)
The Big Top Variety Show (Thames)
The Paul Daniels Magic Show (BBC)
The Royal Fireworks (BBC)
The Royal Wedding (BBC)

TOP TV MOVIES, 1981

		audience millions
1	*Jaws* (ITV)	23.25
2	*Diamonds Are Forever* (ITV)	22.15
3	*Rollercoaster* (ITV)	18.85
4	*Death Wish* (ITV)	15.95

No other movies reached the Top Five monthly placings. Neither did a single sports programme.

SHARE OF TOTAL VIEWING AUDIENCE 1981
(Average monthly figures)

	%
ITV	49.25
BBC1	38.88
BBC 2	11.87

AVERAGE INDIVIDUAL'S DAILY VIEWING

	hours
Watching ITV	1.69
BBC 1	1.29
BBC 2	0.39
Total	3.37 hours

Letters to *Points of View*

Points of View is the BBC television programme which for the last twenty years has been allowing us to share what viewers think of programmes. The current presenter is Barry Took. On the twentieth aniversary of the programme, he described in the *Daily Mail* the sort of correspondence he and the programme get.

'. . . You have a bad sense of humour and wear dull BBC wardrobes which look more like Oxfam rejects.'

This was one of the letters I opened recently. In another, a lady from Rochdale told me that if she had a voice like mine she would shoot herself.

Well, if I were a woman, so would I.

But I'm not the only victim. Hearing that Michael Parkinson had signed a million-pound contract to appear in Australia for six months of the year, one viewer suggested starting a fund to send him there full time.

Angela Rippon, much loved as a newsreader, went down in the estimation of many when she branched out. A lady wrote about Miss Rippon's programme, *The Psychic Business*: 'What a pity that such an absorbing, serious and intriguing subject was reduced to the level of a third-rate woman's magazine article on an off week. Pull your socks up, Angela!'

But if Angela Rippon can, at times, make the viewers cross, they boil with rage at the sight of . . . well, guess who.

'We wish to complain most vigorously about that awful woman with the teeth.' Thus three law students writing from Guildford. And a lady from Castle Bromwich says she finds Esther Rantzen's 'patronizing attitude to the older generation distasteful and thoughtless'.

Our viewers do have their heroes too: David Attenborough is one, David Bellamy another. Richard Baker is much liked, and I've never read a cross word about Kenneth Kendall.'

Points of View Top Ten

Barry Took says: 'If I had to devise a Top Ten according to correspondents, it would come out something like this:

1 *Life on Earth*
2 *The World About Us*
3 Any programme of light music
4 *To Serve Them All My Days* (whether it's on or not)
5 *Crown Green Bowling*
6 *Dallas*
7 *Blake's Seven*
8 Any show-jumping event
9 *Blue Peter*
10 *The Professionals* (I know it's on ITV but it's nonetheless a winner with our correspondents)

TENNIS

1982 British rankings

Last year's rankings appear in brackets.

Men

1	C. J. Mottram (Surrey)	(1)
2	R. A. Lewis (Middx)	(7)
3	J. R. Smith (Devon)	(3)
4	J. M. Lloyd (Essex)	(—)
5	J. W. Feaver (Dorset)	(4)
6	M. J. Bates (Surrey)	(10)
7	A. M. Jarrett (Derbys)	(6)
8	J. M. Dier (Sussex)	(11)
9	N. C. Sears (Sussex)	(19)
10	J. Whiteford (Sussex)	(9)

Women

1	S. Barker (Devon)	(2)
2	S. V. Wade (Kent)	(1)
3	J. M. Durie (Avon)	(4)
4	A. E. Hobbs (Cheshire)	(3)
5	G. L. Coles (Middx)	(9)
6	D. A. Jevans (Essex)	(5)
7	K. J. Brasher (Surrey)	(6)
8	L. J. Charles (Hereford and Worcs)	(7)
9	A. P. Cooper (Kent)	(8)
10	E. S. Jones (Hants and Isle of Wight)	(13)

TINGLES

Godfrey Smith delighted the readers of his column in the *Sunday Times* by asking them to write in to him with their suggestions for favourite place names, pieces of music, words and so on. These will be collected in full in a book *Beyond the Tingle Quotient,* to be published by Weidenfeld and Nicolson in late 1982. In the meantime, here are a few of his lists . . .

The Tingle Quotient

Everyone has a favourite piece of music that makes the hairs on the back of their necks stand up, perhaps because of one sublime moment in the piece. Public consensus provided ten compositions rich in Tingle Quotient.

1 **The St Matthew Passion** – Bach
2 **Der Rosenkavalier** (particularly the last act) – Richard Strauss
3 **Mass in B Minor** – Bach
4 **Marriage of Figaro** – Mozart
5 **Miserere** – Allegri

6   **Cello Concerto** (particularly as played by Jacqueline du Pré) – Elgar
7   **The Dream of Gerontius** (particularly the final movement) – Elgar
8   **Piano Concerto 21** – Mozart
9   **Liebestod** from **Tristan und Isolde** – Wagner
10 { **The Fauré Requiem**
    { **Symphony No 5** – Mahler

Godfrey Smith did not include any popular songs in his list. So we asked David Thomas for his list of Rock Tingles, in no particular order of merit.

Rock Tingles

1   **Blue Suede Shoes** – as written by Carl Perkins and performed by Elvis Presley; still exciting and fresh more than a quarter of a century on.
2   **Jumping Jack Flash** – The Rolling Stones, particularly the live version, although *Satisfaction, Brown Sugar* and many others run it close. Again sheer excitement is the reason for its choice.
3   **I Think It's Going To Work Out Fine** – Ry Cooder; a beautiful instrumental to soothe even the most troubled spirit.
4   **I've Been Loving You Too Long** – Otis Redding; soul music at its most passionate and moving, sung with astonishing control as well as feeling.
5   **Duncan** – Paul Simon; for melodic beauty matched with lyric wit and melancholy there has been no one to touch Paul Simon since Cole Porter (dare one say that Simon is the greater of the two)? *Duncan* is an entirely personal choice; *Still Crazy After All These Years, 50 Ways to Leave Your Lover, Mrs Robinson* – any one of twenty would have done as well.

6 **My Girl** – Smokey Robinson; another writer of beautiful songs. *Tracks Of My Tears* is another classic that comes to mind.

7 **Girl** – The Beatles; the way that Lennon's voice catches as he sings the chorus has always sent shivers down my spine.

8 **Follow That Dream** – as sung by Bruce Springsteen; this is an old Presley song, when Springsteen sings it in concert it sums up all the sense of hope, determination and faith that makes him such an inspiring performer.

9 **Let's Get It On** – Marvin Gaye; simply the sexiest song ever.

10 **The End** – The Doors; apocalyptic, Oedipal, psychedelic – how the Doors came up with this 11-minute epic on their first record, at a time (1967) when no one had produced anything remotely similar, goodness only knows, but it still possesses a unique intensity.

Honourable mentions for *Lately* by Stevie Wonder, and *Chances Are*, the original version of which, sung by a young Bob Marley to a continuous solo saxophone backing, can bring tears to any eyes.

Yet another list could be composed to cover the singing of Sinatra and Fitzgerald, the compositions of Porter, Gershwin et al. In the meantime, you could work out your own tingle list, ranging through all the sensations (but keep it clean), and we might publish it in a future *Book of British Lists*.

TOYS

Best-selling toys, 1981
National Association of Toy Retailers

in order of sales
1 Rubik Cube
2 Star Wars figures

3 Sindy Doll and accessories
4 Lego
5 Astro Wars
6 Action Man
7 Rubik Snake Puzzle
8 Connect 4
9 Britains Farm & Space figures
10 Kensington

TRADE UNIONS

Trade union membership, 1979

SSRC industrial relations research unit

industry	potential union membership (thousands)	percentage belonging to trade union
Metals and engineering	3 833	79
Local government and education	2 893	81
Distribution	2 849	15
Construction	1 420	37
Health	1 321	74
Hotels and catering	973	8
Insurance, banking and finance	925	45
Food, drink and tobacco	729	65
Central government	653	93
Paper, print and publishing	556	83
Road transport	445	100
Post and telecommunications	428	99
Clothing and footwear	388	50

industry	potential union membership (thousands)	percentage belonging to trade union
Agriculture, horticulture and forestry	368	22
Gas, electricity and water	355	98
Coal mining	306	97
Railways	213	95
Sea transport	85	96
Port and inland water transport	70	90
Fishing	11	19

UNDERGROUND

Disused Underground stations

Except for *Osterley Park* which is on the surface, all these old stations are under ground – either bricked up or lurking under a layer of dust just out of sight along the tunnels. The street entrances of some of them can still be found. London Transport did not admit to running any ghost trains . . .

Central Line	*British Museum*	Near *Tottenham Court Road*
	Post Office	Near *St Pauls*
District Line	*Mark Lane*	Near *Tower Hill*
	St Mary's	Between *Aldgate East* and *Whitechapel*
Metropolitan Line	*Marlborough*	Between *Baker Street* and *Finchley Road*
	St John's Wood Road	
Northern Line	*City Road*	Between *Angel* and *Old Street*
Piccadilly Line	*Brompton Road*	Between *Knightsbridge* and *South Kensington*
	Down Street	Between *Hyde Park Corner* and *Green Park*
	Osterley Park	Near *Osterley*

UNEMPLOYMENT IN THE UK

DoE

	thousands	unemployment rate %
1961	346	1.5
1966	361	1.5
1971	792	3.5
1976	1 359	5.7
1977	1 484	6.2
1978	1 475	6.1
1979	1 390	5.7
1980	1 795	7.4
1981	2 295	9.5

Just under one third of the 2.3 million registered unemployed in 1981 were women. In April 1981, 50 per cent of the total unemployed had been out of work for over six months. Throughout the 1970s, the South-east has always had the lowest rate and Northern Ireland the highest. Unemployment is lowest among those born in Europe or the Old Commonwealth. Highest rates are amongst those born in the West Indies, East Africa, Pakistan or Bangladesh.

By February 1982, the total had jumped to over 3 million unemployed, with no signs of it coming down significantly.

UNIVERSITY

British university admittances, 1981-82
UCCA

In October 1981, 3% fewer students were accepted at British universities despite a 4% increase in applications. These are the subjects being studied and how hard it was to get in:

subject	no. of applicants 1981	% 1981 applicants accepted for preferred subject	successful home applicants (1980) with 2 Bs and an A or better (rank order in brackets)
1 Accountancy	3 158	20	23* (13)
2 Veterinary science	1 421	21	96* (1)
3 Education	3 524	22	9 (23)
4 Business management	4 740	23	5 (27)
5 Pharmacy	2 599	25	9 (23)
6 Dentistry	2 819	31	18 (19)
7 Architecture	1 867	32	21* (17)
7 Computer science	5 062	32	34 (4)
9 Art and design	1 511	33	23* (13)
10 Medicine	10 810	34	59 (2)
11 Biology	3 596	35	8 (25)
12 Law	8 815	36	38 (3)
12 Mechanical eng	4 755	36	23 (13)
14 Electrical eng	7 367	37	26 (10)
14 Economics	3 667	37	16 (20)
14 Psychology	3 497	37	16 (20)
17 Sociology	2 668	39	4 (28)
18 Civil eng	3 823	40	16 (20)
18 Agriculture	1 412	40	8* (25)
20 English	7 133	41	33 (7)
21 Biochemistry	1 488	43	24 (12)
22 Geography	4 409	44	22 (16)
22 French	1 950	44	25 (25)
24 Music	1 413	46	20* (18)
25 History	4 381	53	30 (8)
26 Mathematics	4 327	61	34 (4)
26 Physics	3 406	61	34 (4)
28 Chemistry	3 186	62	30 (8)
Total (all subjects)	167 096	37	26

Accountancy overtook veterinary science as the most difficult subject on which to enter university, as judged by the proportion of applicants accepted to study the subject of their choice. Only one in five accountancy applicants were successful, compared with an overall success rate for all subjects of 37 per cent.

However, veterinary science still requires by far the most difficult qualifications. Figures for university entrants in 1980, the latest available, show that 96 per cent of those accepted to read veterinary science had at least two A-level passes at grade B and an A or better.

The table, complied from the UCCA statistics, ranks subjects according to their difficulty in terms of the proportion of candidates who get into the subject of their choice.

The figures in brackets in the final column ranks subjects according to their difficulty in terms of A-level grades.

VACCINES

Kendig and Hutton: Lifespans

disease	effective lifespan of vaccination
Smallpox (cowpox virus)	5–10 years
Diphtheria (toxid)	5–10 years
Diphtheria (antitoxin)	2–3 months
Typhoid (dead germs)	2–3 years
Whooping cough (dead germs)	2–5 years
Measles (attenuated virus)	many years
Tetanus (toxid)	5–10 years
Tetanus (antitoxin)	few weeks
Poliomyelitis (dead or attenuated virus)	unknown
Rubella (attenuated virus)	unknown

VALENTINES

Women whom men would like to spend St Valentine's Day with

1 Sophia Loren
2 Pamela Stephenson
3 Margaret Thatcher

Yes, seriously, Mrs Thatcher did get on the list, but she scored only 3%, most of them pensioners who said they would rather spend a day with her than with their wives.

Men whom women would like to spend St Valentine's Day with

1 Terry Wogan
2 Roger Moore
3 Prince Charles
4 Sting (of The Police pop group)

These results were from a survey published in the London evening *Standard*. The vast majority of people asked did *not* want to spend St Valentine's Day with their regular partners – wives and girlfriends scored 7% and husbands and boyfriends only 6%. More men than women send Valentine cards and more Southerners than Northerners.

The survey, which was carried out by a mouthwash manufacturer, also asked about kissing.

Kissing

	%
Kissed someone on the mouth in the last week	79
Kissed someone on the mouth in the last 24 hours	53
Can't remember when last kissed someone on the mouth	16

Scots kiss least – 9% below the national average.

VASECTOMIES

Vasectomies performed in clinics in the UK

	Social trends	
	1975	1980
patient's age	%	%
under 25	2	2
25–29	23	19
30 and over	66	76
not stated	10	3

The total number of vasectomies performed fell from 18 600 in 1975 to 14 400 in 1980.

VEGETARIANS

Seven famous vegetarians

1 George Bernard Shaw (1856–1950) playwright
2 Percy Bysshe Shelley (1792–1822) poet
3 Roger McGough   (1937–   ) poet
4 Marty Feldman   (1933–   ) actor
5 George Harrison   (1943–   ) singer
6 Peter Sellers   (1925–1980) actor
7 Twiggy   (1949–   ) actress

VIDEO

Top ten video movies
Video Business

More and more people are going to the cinema in their own living rooms as more and more up-to-date films become available on video cassette. Here are the most popular video movies sold in 1981.

1 *The Life of Brian* – Thorn/EMI
2 *The Jazz Singer* – Thorn/EMI
3 *The Elephant Man* – Thorn/EMI
4 *Brubaker* – 20th Century Fox
5 *The Long Good Friday* – Thorn/EMI
6 *Shogun Assassin* – VIPCO
7 *The Last Hunter* – Interlite
8 *The Blue Brothers* – CIC
9 *The Postman Always Rings Twice* – Guild
10 *Flash Gordon* – Thorn/EMI

VOLUNTARY ORGANIZATIONS

Memberships, 1980

Social Trends

	thousands
National Trust (except Scotland)	1 055
Royal British Legion	916
National Association of Leagues of Hospital Friends	457
National Federation of Women's Institutes	384
British Red Cross	114
National Union of Townswomens Guilds	180
St John Ambulance Brigade	79
Rotary International	60
National Association of Round Tables	31
Lion's Clubs	19
Toc H	11

WINE

European comparison of consumption, in litres per head per year, 1978-79

Eurostat

France	94	West Germany	24
Italy	86	Belgium/Luxembourg	19
Portugal	83	Denmark	13
Spain	59	Netherlands	12
Greece	45	Sweden	9
Switzerland	40	UK	8
Austria	35	Ireland	3

WOMEN

British Women Composers

A list compiled for us by Joe Herkes of Enfield.

Arthur, Fanny (*c.* 1820–79)
Barnard, Mrs (1830–69)
Bright, Dora (1863–1952)
Dunlop, Isobel (1901–75)
Gipps, Ruth (*b.* 1921)
Hardelot, Guy d' (pseudonym of Helen Rhodes) (1859–1936)
Holst, Imogen (*b.* 1907)
Howell, Dorothy (*b.* 1898)
Lutyens, Elisabeth (*b.* 1906)
Maconchy, Elizabeth (*b.* 1907)
Musgrave, Thea (*b.* 1928)
Poston, Elizabeth (*b.* 1905)
Savage, Jane (active 1785–95)
Smyth, Dame Ethel (1858–1944)
Tate, Phyllis Margaret Duncan (*b.* 1911)
Taylor, Mrs Tom (nee Laura W. Barker) (1819–1905)
White, Maude Valerie (1855–1937)
Wilkins, Margaret Lucy (*b.* 1941)
Williams, Grace (*b.* 1941)
Woodford-Finden-Ward, Amy (Late Victorian)
'Zenta Hermann' (pseudonym of Augusta May Ann Holmes: French/Irish) (1847–1903)

WORDS

Philip Howard's most misused words, 1982

Philip Howard, Literary Editor of *The Times* and arbiter of the world of words, offers his list of the most misused words in English in 1982, with commentary, of course . . .

'Misused' is a fighting word. The language belongs to all of us who use it. And if enough of us decide to use a word in a different way, the different way becomes its 'correct' meaning. If words were glued irremovably to their original meanings, we should still be using 'nice' to mean stupid, and 'meat' to mean any sort of food, not just the food of carnivores. But here are some of the most misunderstood and misused words; or, if you take a calmer, more rational view of language, words the meanings of which are changing rapidly.

hopefully
disinterested
decimate
internecine
literally
massive/minuscule
tragedy (in sport)
refute
flaunt/flout

Philip Howard also points to historically incorrect references to King Canute. Poor old Canute was *not* trying to turn back the tide but demonstrating to sycophantic courtiers precisely that he *couldn't* and was *not* all-powerful. But perhaps it's too late to rehabilitate him now.

WORK

Average hours worked weekly in Europe

European Commission: labour force survey, 1979

full time workers	men	women
Ireland	49.1	40.0
France	45.0	42.0
UK	43.8	37.5
West Germany	43.7	41.9
Belgium	43.1	41.1
Netherlands	42.6	36.4
Denmark	42.5	38.6
Luxembourg	42.2	41.3
Italy	41.9	38.6

Average hours have decreased everywhere since 1977.

Zs

The last ten surnames in the London telephone directory

Zylinska   Zytnik
Zyms   Zywczyk
Zysblat   Zyzniewski
Zyskowski   Zzaman
Zysman   Zzitz

Now you can go to Zzzzz . . .

Ireland

The following section consists of lists to do with Ireland, both North and South. We thought by now that someone would have brought out a Book of Irish Lists, and Scottish Lists and Welsh Lists, but apparently not. We do like to help.

POPULATION

REPUBLIC OF IRELAND 3 368 217
1979 census

Chief cities

Dublin	544 586
Cork	138 267
Limerick	60 665
Dun Laoghaire	54 244
Galway	36 917
Waterford	32 617

NORTHERN IRELAND 1 538 800
Latest official Government estimates

Chief cities

Belfast	354 400
Derry	87 900

RELIGIONS

Latest official Government estimates

IRISH REPUBLIC	%
Catholic	94
Church of Ireland	3.3
Presbyterian	0.5
Methodist	0.2
Others	2

NORTHERN IRELAND	%
Catholic	31.4
Presbyterian	26.7
Church of Ireland	22
Methodist	4.7
Others	5.8
Not stated	9.4

IRISH SUPERLATIVES

Longest river	Shannon (240 miles)
Largest freshwater lake	Lough Neagh (150 sq miles)
Highest cliffs	Croaghan, Achill Island, Co Mayo (2192 feet)
Highest mountain	Carrantuohill, Co Kerry (3414 ft)
Deepest cave	Carrowmore Cavern, Co Mayo (495 ft)
Highest waterfall	Powerscourt Falls, Co Wicklow (350 ft)
Tallest tree	Sitka spruce at Curraghmore, Waterford (166 ft)
Longest place-name	Muckanaghederdauhaulia (22 letters), Co Galway (*meaning:* 'soft place between two seas')

Oldest castle	Ferrycarrig, near Wexford (c. 1180)
Oldest pub	The Brazen Head, Dublin (licensed 1666)
Longest bar	The Grand Stand Bar, Galway Racecourse (210 ft)

FAMOUS ARRIVALS

432: St Patrick. He brought the Christian faith to Ireland, establishing his episcopal see at Armagh, where it still remains. According to legend, he used the shamrock to teach the doctrine of the Trinity and drove all snakes out of Ireland.

795: The Vikings. The northern raiders steadily increased their power in Ireland over the next two centuries, founding settlements at Dublin, Waterford and Limerick. They were finally defeated by King Brian Boru at the Battle of Clontarf, north of Dublin, in 1014.

1169: The Normans. The tortured 800-year relationship between Ireland and England began when Henry II got a Papal Bull from the English Pope Adrian to put Ireland in order. Most of the Irish kings quickly submitted to Norman rule, with the exception of the O'Neills and O'Donnells of the North. In due course the Normans were absorbed to such a degree that they became 'more Irish than the Irish themselves'. Norman names characteristically bear the prefix Fitz-, as in Fitzpatrick, Fitzsimons or Fitzgerald.

1608: The Ulster 'planters'. The English Crown seized most of the land in Ulster, ejected the native Catholic landholders and replaced them with 150 000 Scottish Presbyterians and 50 000 English Protestants. This sowed the seed for the partitioning of Ireland in the present century and the conflicts that have resulted from it.

1649: Oliver Cromwell. A decade of insurrection ended when Cromwell landed with his New Model Army and crushed all resistance with a severity that is resented even today. All 3000 defenders and inhabitants of the town of Drogheda were put to the sword.

1690: William of Orange. The Battle of the Boyne, at which the Dutch Protestant William defeated the English Catholic James II, is celebrated annually on 12 July, the chief date in the Ulster loyalist calendar. However, the event had more to do with European than Irish politics; ironically, William's victory was greeted with joy in the Vatican.

1919: Sir John Alcock and Sir Arthur Whitten Brown. They landed near Clifden, Co Galway, 16 hours and 27 minutes after take-off in Newfoundland, to complete the first non-stop transatlantic flight.

1963: President John F. Kennedy. The first US leader to pay an official visit to Ireland, where his photograph shared pride of place in many households with that of the Pope.

1980: Pope John Paul II: The biggest crowds ever seen in the country turned out for the first ever papal visit. His main appeal was for peace – but many ears remain deaf to his words.

UNCOMPLIMENTARY REMARKS ABOUT IRELAND

'. . . there is hardly a city in the world that entertains such variety of devil's imps as Dublin doth. If any knavishly break, murder, rob or are desirous of polygamy, they straightway repair thither, making that place, or the kingdom in general, their asylum, or sanctuary.'

Richard Head (c. 1600)

'The Irish are a fair people – they never speak well of one another.'

Samuel Johnson

'No nation in Europe is less given to industry or is more phlegmatic than this. They do not concern themselves with ecclesiastical or political amelioration.'
Giovanni Battista Rinuccini, papal nuncio (1645)

'Being born in a stable does not make one a horse.'
The Duke of Wellington, who was born in Dublin, on being asked if he was therefore an Irishman

'Ireland is the old sow that eats her farrow.'
Stephen Dedalus, James Joyce's alter ego, in Portrait of the Artist as a Young Man

HISTORIC IRISH QUOTATIONS

'I met with Napper Tandy, and he took me by the hand,
And he said, "How's poor ould Ireland, and how does she stand?"
"She's the most distressful country that ever yet was seen,
For they're hanging men and women there for the Wearin' o' the Green."'
Popular ballad (18th century)

'Let no man write my epitaph . . . Let my memory be left in oblivion, and my tomb remain uninscribed, until other times and other men can do justice to my character. When my country takes her place among the nations of the earth, then, and not till then, let my epitaph be written.'
Robert Emmet's speech from the dock (1803)

'No man has the right to fix the boundary to the march of a nation. No man has a right to say to his country, thus far shalt thou go and no further.'
Charles Stuart Parnell

'Ulster will fight and Ulster will be right.'
>   *Lord Randolph Churchill (1886)*

'Ireland unfree shall never be at peace.'
>   *Patrick Pearse*

'Home rule is Rome rule.'
>   *Popular Unionist slogan*

'Romantic Ireland's dead and gone.'
It's with O'Leary in the grave,'
>   *W. B. Yeats, September 1913*

'All changed, changed utterly:
A terrible beauty is born.'
>   *W. B. Yeats, Easter 1916*

'All I boast is that we are a Protestant parliament and a Protestant state.'
>   *James Craig, first Prime Minister of Northern Ireland (1934)*

'Ulster stands at the crossroads.'
>   *Terence O'Neill, Prime Minister of Northern Ireland (1968)*

GREAT IRISH PLAYWRIGHTS

1   William Congreve (1670–1729): *The Way of the World*
2   Oliver Goldsmith (1728–74): *She Stoops to Conquer*
3   Richard Brinsley Sheridan (1751–1816): *The Rivals, The School for Scandal, The Critic*
4   Oscar Wilde (1854–1900): *Lady Windermere's Fan, The Importance of Being Earnest, Salome*

TEN EPIGRAMS BY OSCAR WILDE

1 'The English country gentleman galloping after a fox – the unspeakable in pursuit of the uneatable.'

2 'A cynic is a man who knows the price of everything, and the value of nothing.'

3 'I have nothing to declare but my genius.' (*To the US customs*)

4 '. . . I have put my genius into my life – I have put only my talent into my works.'

5 'Work is the curse of the drinking classes.'

6 'I have the simplest tastes. I am always satisfied with the best.'

7 '. . . your Scotsman believes only in success. How can a man who regards success as the goal of life be a true artist?'

8 'I was thinking in bed this morning that the great superiority of France over England is that in France every bourgeois wants to be an artist, whereas in England every artist wants to be a bourgeois.'

9 'The only thing to do with good advice is to pass it on.'

10 'Art should never try to be popular. The public should try to make itself artistic.'

US PRESIDENTS OF IRISH DESCENT

Andrew Jackson (President from 1829–1837)
James Knox Polk (1845–49)
James Buchanan (1857–61)
Andrew Johnson (1865–69)
Ulysses Grant (1869–77)
Chester Arthur (1881–85)
Grover Cleveland (1885–89, 1893–97)
Benjamin Harrison (1889–93)
William McKinley (1893–1901)
Woodrow Wilson (1913–21)
John F. Kennedy (1960–63)
Ronald Reagan (1980–   )

With the exception of Kennedy, whose ancestors came from New Ross, Co Wexford, and Reagan (Ballyporeen, Co. Tipperary), all of these presidents were descended from emigrants from the province of Ulster.

Richard Nixon and Jimmy Carter also unearthed Irish ancestors, but the links are more tenuous – and they also had elections coming up.

THE AER LINGUS FLEET, 1982
(named after Irish saints)

Boeing 747s   St Patrick
St Ciaran
St Colmcille

Boeing 737s	St Jarlath
	St Ailbhe
	St Macartan
	St Ide
	St Fachtna
	St Naithi
	St Cormac
	St Eugene
	St Killian
	St Oliver Plunkett
	St Eunan
	St Fiachre
BAC 1-11s	St Mel
	St Malachy
	St Declan
	St Ronan

FAMOUS IRISH EXPORTS

Guinness
Whiskeys (Jameson, Paddy, Power's, Bushmills)
Waterford crystal
Connemara marble
Aran knitwear
Linen
Beleek pottery
Donegal tweed
Dublin Bay lobsters
Racehorses
Kerrygold butter
Peterson pipes
James Joyce
John McCormack
George Best

THE IRISH REPUBLIC'S TOP TEN EXPORTS, 1979

	£
Food, drink and tobacco (excluding meat)	711 370 574
Machinery and transport equipment	561 199 025
Meat and meat preparations	451 906 705
Chemicals	451 699 920
Textiles	234 112 717
Livestock	131 451 018
Clothing and footwear	117 541 322
Professional and scientific goods	111 037 044
Metals and manufactures	105 187 751
Metal ores and scrap	77 931 324

RESTAURANTS
Irish restaurants awarded stars in the Egon Ronay Guide, 1982

Three stars
Arbutus Lodge Hotel, Cork
One star
The Barn, Saintfield, Co Down
Ballylickey House Hotel, Ballylickey, Co Cork
Cashel Palace Hotel, Cashel, Co Tipperary
Chez Hans, Cashel
Ashford Castle, Cong, Co Mayo

VISITORS
Visitors to Northern Ireland

1959	633 000
1963	704 000
1967	1 080 000
1968	1 139 000
1972	435 000
1978	628 100
1979	728 000
1980	710 000

The number of visitors to Northern Ireland has been increasing over the last eight years, despite all the Troubles. Their best year was in 1968 when the province attracted well over a million tourists. Numbers fell dramatically when the Troubles began, dropping to 435 000 in 1972. But since then, there has been a gradual return, though the traffic is nowhere as busy as it was before.

A visitor, for the sake of these figures, is defined as someone spending seven nights or more in the province. Most of them came from England, 43%, followed by the Irish Republic 31%, Scotland 11%, North America 7½%, and Europe 4%.

The majority of these outside visitors, 56%, were on trips to stay with friends or relations, while 25% were on business. Nonetheless, there were still many people going to Northern Ireland for pure pleasure – 16%. It is of course a beautiful place. Here are some of the sights they all visited.

Tourist attraction admissions in Northern Ireland

		1979 admissions
1	Crawfordsburn Country Park	200 000
2	Ulster Folk & Transport Museum	145 635
3	Tollymore Forest Park	129 000
4	Giant's Causeway	120 000

5	Castlewellan Forest Park	72 000
6	Ulster American Folk Park	55 348
7	Armagh Planetarium	50 000
8	Glenarrif Forest Park	49 000
9	Gortin Glen Forest Park	39 000
10	Carrickfergus Castle	39 000
11	Gosford Forest Park	29 000
12	Shanes Castle Railway/Nature Reserve	28 000
13	Castleward (National Trust)	27 290
14	Drum Manor Forest Park	25 000

The Republic's top ten tourist attractions

Irish Tourist Board

1 Blarney Castle, Co Cork
2 Bunratty Castle and Folk Park, Co Clare
3 Rock of Cashel, Co Tipperary
4 Craggaunowen Castle, Co Clare
5 Glendalough, Co Wicklow
6 John F. Kennedy Park, New Ross, Co Wexford
7 Killarney and the Ring of Kerry
8 Lough Key Forest Park, Co Roscommon
9 Newgrange, Co Meath (ancient passage graves)
10 State Apartments, Dublin Castle

TAX EXILES

Irish Embassy, London

In 1969, Ireland's then Minister of Finance, Charles Haughey, introduced a scheme whereby artists living in the Republic would be free of income tax. He was trying to raise the quality of Ireland's cultural life, keeping the artists they had and perhaps encouraging eminent poets, sculptors, composers and suchlike to settle in Ireland from abroad. One of the people he had in mind was Henry Moore – but he never came. Instead, there was a flood of writers, most of them word-shifting, best-selling, mass-producing paperback writers. Several of the following have recently moved on, but many still remain based in Ireland.

Len Deighton
Frederick Forsyth
Alun Owen
Wolf Mankowitz
J. P. Donleavy
Malcolm McDonald
Susan Howatch
Gordon Thomas
Patrick Skene Catling

MOVIES MADE IN IRELAND

1 *The Informer* (1935). Director: John Ford. Thriller set in the 'Troubles', starring Victor McLaglen.
2 *Odd Man Out* (1947). Director: Carol Reed. Stars James Mason as an Irish rebel hunted by police.
3 *The Quiet Man* (1952). John Wayne plays an Irish-American broth of a boy who wins the heart of local colleen Maureen O'Hara.
4 *The March Hare* (1956). Director: George More O'Ferrall. Terence Morgan, Cyril Cusack and Wilfred Hyde White in aery-faery farce about a racehorse.
5 *Rooney* (1958). Director: George Pollock. John Gregson stars in rags-to-riches rubbish. Aptly, he plays a dustman.
6 *Young Cassidy* (1965). Directors: John Ford/Jack Cardiff. Rod Taylor ludicrously miscast as Sean O'Casey, with Julie Christie and Maggie Smith as his women.
7 *The Blue Max* (1965). Director: John Guillermin. A stirring yarn, with George Peppard and Jeremy Kemp as

rival World War I German flying aces, James Mason as their clinical and cynical CO, and Ursula Andress in undress.

8 *Ulysses* (1967). Director: Joseph Strick. Milo O'Shea as Leopold Bloom, Barbara Jefford as Molly, in honest attempt to put Joyce's stream of consciousness on the screen.

9 *Darling Lilli* (1969). Director: Blake Edwards. Julie Andrews and Rock Hudson in would-be spy comedy that flopped famously.

10 *Ryan's Daughter* (1970). Director: David Lean. Love-triangle story set on the Dingle Peninsula in 1916. Robert Mitchum, Sarah Miles and Christopher Jones star. John Mills won an Oscar for his playing of the village idiot but the best performances come from the sea and the scenery.

11 *The Mackintosh Man* (1973). Director: John Huston. Wet thriller starring Paul Newman, James Mason and Dominique Sanda.

12 *Zardoz* (1973). Director: John Boorman. Sean Connery and Charlotte Rampling in strange, futuristic fantasy amid the Wicklow Mountains.

13 *Excalibur* (1981). Director: John Boorman. The Arthurian legend quirkily retold, with Nigel Terry as a bemused king and Nicol Williamson as a highly-mannered Merlin.

PROFESSIONAL IRISHMEN

Dave Allen
Eamonn Andrews
Frank Delaney
Val Doonican
James Galway
Richard Harris
Henry Kelly
Peter O'Toole
Terry Wogan

The order is alphabetical only, but they are all terribly Irish, and proud of it, making it part of their trade mark. Another common denominator is that none of them lives in Ireland.

Scotland

POPULATION

1971 census

Total population 5.2 million

Cities
Glasgow	794 316
Edinburgh	455 126
Aberdeen	208 569
Dundee	190 793

Districts (under local government reorganization)
Renfrew (Paisley)	213 188
Motherwell	150 857
Kirkcaldy	149 000
Falkirk	145 000
Cunninghame (Irvine)	135 703
West Lothian (Bathgate)	132 242
Dunfermline	126 504
Perth and Kinross	119 470
Kyle and Carrick (Ayr)	112 000
Monkland (Coatbridge)	109 645
Inverclyde (Greenock)	109 000
Hamilton	107 000

WATERWAYS

Main rivers

Clyde (106 miles) – great shipbuilding river flowing through Glasgow and Clydebank, where the Queen Mary, Queen Elizabeth and QE2 were built

Tweed (96 miles) – valley of Scotland's woollen industry, entering the sea at Berwick

Tay (117 miles) – Scotland's longest river, famed for its salmon. Flows under road and rail bridges as it reaches the sea at Dundee

Dee (90 miles) – salmon river of gentle beauty, giving its name to Royal Deeside and flowing past Balmoral on way to Aberdeen

Spey (110 miles) – Scotland's swiftest river, also famed for its salmon, flows northwards to the Moray Firth, reaching it at Spey Bay by Garmouth

Forth (66 miles) – flowing eastward by Edinburgh to the North Sea; well known for its two famous bridges, one road, one rail, which cross from the Lothians to Fife.

Lochs

Loch Lomond (24 miles) – Scotland's biggest loch, situated less than 20 miles from Glasgow and famous for its song

Loch Ness – famous for its Monster, is also 24 miles long, running from Inverness to Fort Augustus

ISLANDS WITH SMALLEST POPULATION

Last census

	inhabitants
Dry	2
Eilean Donan	2
Tanera Mor	2
Ensay	2
Killegray	2
Carna	3
Papa Stronsay	3
Swona	3
Noss	3
Eilean Na Cille	4
Grimsay	4
Pabbay	4

TEN HIGHEST SCOTTISH MOUNTAINS

	height in feet
Ben Nevis	4406
Ben Macdui	4300
Braeriach	4248
Cairn Toul	4241
Cairngorm	4084
Aonach Beag	4060
Carn Mor Dearg	4012
Aonach Mor	3999
Ben Lawers	3984
Beinn A'Bhuird	3924

DRAMATIC EVENTS IN SCOTTISH HISTORY

David I founds Holyrood Abbey (1128)

David, out hunting on the skirts of Arthur's Seat (near Edinburgh), was attacked by a wounded stag. His horse bolted and threw him and, half stunned, the King was in danger of being gored when his only companion, a chaplain, swung the casket on a chain he carried with the fragment of the True Cross, or Holy Rood, before the beast's face. It drew off in alarm and the King was saved. In thankfulness, David vowed that he would build an abbey on the spot, to be called the Abbey of the Holy Rood. In time, the royal palace developed alongside.

Edward I of England sacks Berwick (1296)
When Edward I, in his campaign to make himself Lord Paramount of Scotland, came north in force, he decided to make an example of Berwick-on-Tweed, then Scotland's greatest sea-port, to discourage later resistance. He took the city by storm and massacred no fewer than 17 000 men, women and children, ordering the bodies to be left lying in the streets as a warning to the rest of Scotland. Considering that the total population of Berwick today is about 13 000, you get some idea of the scale of the horror.

The Declaration of Arbroath (1320)
One of the most noble documents ever produced, on which the American Declaration of Independence is largely based, was written and signed at Arbroath Abbey six years after Bannockburn, as a letter to the Pope, proclaiming the nation's undying devotion to freedom and stating how the Scots would even get rid of their own beloved hero-king, Robert Bruce, if he should fail to respect their liberties; and vowing that, so long as one hundred of them remained alive, they would fight to save the nation's independence. The Declaration is still preserved in Edinburgh, signed by the leadership of Scotland in great numbers and assented to by Bruce himself.

Black Agnes of Dunbar (1338)
In the troubled reign of young David II, Bruce's son, Dunbar Castle was besieged by English invaders under Salisbury. The Earl of Dunbar and March was absent but the castle was held by his countess, Black Agnes. She held out for over five months and used to wipe away the dust and fragments from hits by cannon-balls with white napkins, to the great annoyance of the cannoneers. At length the English tired of the siege and went away.

James II and the Earl of Douglas (1452)
Perhaps the only occasion when a monarch acted as his own assassin. James II, much fearing the power of the Douglases,

invited the young 8th Earl to Stirling Castle, under safe-conduct, and there personally stabbed him to death, before all his court. The King himself was blown up by a bursting cannon at Roxburgh four years later.

Murder of Cardinal Beaton (1546)

A group of Protestant adherents, led by the Master of Rothes and James Melville, burst into Cardinal David Beaton's bed-chamber at St Andrews and stabbed him. In the middle of it, Melville held up his hand and cried 'Halt! This is not being done godly. Let us pray!' So they knelt and prayed, then rose and finished off the Cardinal and hung his naked body out of the window. Beaton, who was both Primate of Holy Church and Chancellor of the Realm, or chief minister, had been ruling Scotland for long and had almost personally held up the Reformation for years. This deed finally ushered in the establishment of the Reformation.

GREAT SCOTS

Great Scot, what would the world have done without them. Just look at some of their discoveries, inventions, creations and achievements:

Television	John Logie Baird
Telephone	Alexander Graham Bell
Penicillin	Alexander Fleming
Chloroform	James Simpson
The waterproof	Charles Mackintosh
The thermos flask	James Dewar
Marmalade	Mrs Keiller of Dundee
Radar	Robert Watson Watt
Shale-oil	James 'Paraffin' Young
The Labour Party	Keir Hardie
The American Navy	John Paul Jones
The historical novel	Walter Scott

The bicycle	Kirkpatrick Macmillan (a blacksmith from Thornhill, Dumfries)
Treasure Island	Robert Louis Stevenson
Peter Pan	J. M. Barrie
Sherlock Holmes	Arthur Conan Doyle (born Edinburgh)
Macadamized roads	John McAdam

EVEN MORE SCOTS

James Clerk Maxwell. It is doubtful if one Scot in a hundred would recognize his name, which is a fair measure of a shameful neglect, yet James Clerk Maxwell was one of the greatest of all Scots, a scientific giant to be mentioned in the same breath as Newton and Einstein. He paved the way for everything from television, radio, electricity, radar and space exploration to colour photography. It was his theory of electro-magnetism which brought a scientific revolution and sparked off modern physics.

Earl Haig commanded the British Forces in France in the First World War.

Hugh Dowding masterminded Fighter Command in the Battle of Britain.

Scots Prime Ministers during this century: Henry Campbell-Bannerman, Arthur Balfour, Andrew Bonar Law, Ramsay MacDonald, Harold Macmillan and Alec Douglas-Home.

Henry Lyte wrote 'Abide With Me'.

Lady Nairne gave us 'Will Ye No' Come Back Again?'

Andrew Carnegie in true Scots fashion made one of the world's largest fortunes.

David Livingstone. When American journalist H. M. Stanley went to look for Scots explorer Livingstone, he was sent to the depths of Africa by the *New York Herald*. The *Herald* was founded by James Gordon Bennett. A Scotsman, I presume? Of course. From Banffshire.

ENTERTAINMENT

Gordon Irving's choice of Scotland's 12 greatest comedy entertainers

1 Sir Harry Lauder
2 Will Fyffe
3 Jack Buchanan
4 Tommy Lorne
5 Dave Willis
6 Lex McLean
7 Harry Gordon
8 Stanley Baxter
9 Rikki Fulton
10 Jimmy Logan
11 Jack Milroy
12 Duncan Macrae

Moira Anderson's ten most requested songs

1 *Don't Be Cross*
2 *On a Clear Day*
3 *Vilia*
4 *One Fine Day*
5 *Danny Boy*
6 *The Nuns' Chorus*
7 *My Ain Folk*
8 *Amazing Grace*
9 *The Holy City*
10 *The Skye Boat Song*

Kenneth McKellar's ten favourite Scottish songs

1 *O' My Love is like a Red, Red Rose*
2 *Rowan Tree*
3 *Ae Fond Kiss*
4 *Land o' Heart's Desire*
5 *The Flowers o' the Forest*
6 *Scotland the Brave*
7 *The Road to the Isles*
8 *Kishmul's Galley*
9 *Loch Lomond*
10 *Will Ye No' Come Back Again?*

TEN MOST PROFITABLE PRIVATE SCOTTISH-REGISTERED COMPANIES, 1980

Based on pre-tax profits against net tangible assets

1 J. and G. Stewart Ltd (whisky blenders)   Leith
2 William Sanderson and Son Ltd (whisky blenders) South Queensferry
3 Low Robertson and Co Ltd (whisky merchants) Edinburgh
4 A. and A. Crawford (whisky distillers)   Edinburgh
5 Dundee Fabric (processors of cord and fabric)   Dundee
6 Matthew Gloag and Son (whisky blenders and bottlers)   Perth
7 McFarlane Smith Ltd (manufacturers of fine chemicals)   Edinburgh
8 Robert Sibbald, Travel Agents, Ltd   Edinburgh

9   Parker's Animal Feeds Ltd (manufacturers of animal food compounds)   Glasgow
10 U Save Cash and Carry Ltd (wholesale and general merchants)   Glasgow

NICKY FAIRBAIRN'S PET HATES

By courtesy of the Ex Scottish Solicitor-General:

1   Malice
2   People who think the world owes them homage and the State owes them a living
3   Sociological guilt dressed up as political enlightenment or religious compassion
4   Bores: *animal*   – David Frost
           vegetable   – semolina
           mineral   – modern office architecture
5   Weeds: *animal*   – Wet Lefties
           vegetable   – dandelion
           mineral   – hard and soft drugs
6   Noise: Babies crying, dogs barking, people banging on, punk rock
7   Art-pseuds
8   Centres, precincts, complexes and on-going situations
9   Annabel's in particular and night-clubs in general
10 Nationalized lettering and bowdlerized English
11 Vulgarity, especially souvenirs
12 Non-linen sheets

GOLF

The game which Scotland gave to the world. Now the world gives us a lesson on how to play it.

Ten oldest clubs

1 Royal Burgess Golfing Society of Edinburgh (1735)
2 Bruntsfield Links   (1761)
3 Royal Musselburgh   (1774)
4 Royal Aberdeen   (1780)
5 Crail   (1786)
6 Glasgow   (1787)
7 Dunbar   (1794)
8 Burntisland   (1797)
9 Royal Albert, Montrose   (1810)
10 Scotscraig, Tayport   (1817)

Last ten Open Championships in Scotland

date	location	champion
1980	Muirfield	Tom Watson
1978	St Andrews	Jack Nicklaus
1977	Turnberry	Tom Watson
1975	Carnoustie	Tom Watson
1973	Troon	Tom Weiskopf
1972	Muirfield	Lee Trevino
1970	St Andrews	Jack Nicklaus
1968	Carnoustie	Gary Player
1966	Muirfield	Jack Nicklaus
1964	St Andrews	Tony Lema

Scotland has the highest golf course in Britain – at Leadhills (1500 ft).

Golf courses in Scotland most used for the Open Championship since 1860

Prestwick	24 times
St Andrews	22
Muirfield	12
Musselburgh	6
Carnoustie	5
Troon	5
Turnberry	1

Top Ten Open Championship attendances in Scotland

131 610	Muirfield, 1980
125 271	St Andrews, 1978
87 639	Turnberry, 1977
84 847	Muirfield, 1972
80 044	Troon, 1973
76 142	Carnoustie, 1975
73 147	St Andrews, 1970
51 819	Carnoustie, 1968
40 182	Muirfield, 1966
35 954	St Andrews, 1964

TEN MOST VISITED BUILDINGS OR MONUMENTS IN SCOTLAND, 1980

Edinburgh Castle	919 000
Stirling Castle	364 000
Holyroodhouse	325 000
Cameron House, Loch Lomond	141 000

James Dunn's House, Aberdeen	116 000
Burns' Cottage	106 000
Blair Castle	104 000
Scone Palace	101 000
Culzean Castle	92 000
Cawdor Castle	92 100

TEN OLDEST BOYS' SCHOOLS

George Heriot's, Edinburgh	1628
Hutcheson's Grammar, Glasgow	1641
Robert Gordon's College, Aberdeen	1729
George Watson's College, Edinburgh	1741
Edinburgh Academy	1824
Loretto School, Musselburgh	1827
Daniel Stewart's and Melville College, Edinburgh	1832
Merchiston Castle, Edinburgh	1833
Glenalmond, Perthshire	1841
Glasgow Academy	1845

SOME OF SCOTLAND'S GREATEST DISASTERS

1879: The Tay Bridge – Fierce gales tore a gap in the railway bridge crossing the River Tay, near Dundee, and the North British mail train plunged into the river. With no exact check on who was on board, the death toll was given at between 75 and 90.

1887: Udston Colliery, near Glasgow – An underground fire followed by an explosion brought the deaths of 73 miners.

1905: Watson Street, Glasgow – A fire in a working men's lodging house suffocated 39 and left 32 seriously injured.

1915: Quintins Hill, Dumfries and Galloway – Britain's biggest rail disaster when a triple collision, involving a First World War troop train, brought a death toll of 227.

1929: Paisley Cinema – Two thousand children panicked when trying to escape from a fire at the Glen Cinema, Paisley. The exit-door beside the screen was locked and shuttered – and 70 children died.

1953: The Princess Victoria – The ferry leaving Stranraer for Larne foundered in fierce gales and sank, with the loss of 131 lives.

1959: Auchengeich Colliery – A fire in the coalmine near Chryston, Glasgow, killed 47 miners.

1968: James Watt Street, Glasgow – A fire at a small clothing factory in the heart of Glasgow claimed 22 lives, of both factory staff and firemen.

1971: Ibrox, Glasgow – Scotland's worst football crowd disaster, when 66 spectators died in a crush as they left the Rangers–Celtic match. They were descending towards the exit – on stairway No. 13.

1971: Clarkston, Glasgow – A gas leak at a new shopping centre at Clarkston Toll, on the south side of Glasgow, caused an explosion which killed 20 people.

NIGEL TRANTER'S CHOICE OF SCOTLAND'S MOST RESOUNDING VICTORIES

Largs (1263)
Great victory of Alexander the Third against King Hakon of Norway. It represented the end of Norse and Viking attempts to dominate Scotland. Good tactics and favourable weather conditions against a sea-borne invasion.

Battle of Stirling Bridge (1297)
Although Bannockburn gets the praise as the most significant

Scottish battle, it would not have been possible without Stirling Bridge, 17 years earlier. This was Wallace's greatest achievement, showing Bruce the way. By making splendid use of the terrain and natural features, he demonstrated that it was possible to defeat the overpowering strength of Edward I and the great English war machine.

Battle of Roslin (1303)

Comparatively little known, and a minor battle in some respects, this was a significant step on the way to Bannockburn. It was remarkable in that it comprised three distinct victories in one day, when Sir John Comyn and Sir Simon Fraser defeated three English forces totalling 20 000 men, under some of their senior commanders, on Roslin Moor, with only 8000 Scots.

Bannockburn (1314)

The battle which won Scotland's freedom in the Wars of Independence. Bruce, the hero-king, learning from the dead Wallace, used the marshes of the Forth to bog down the heavy English cavalry, the tanks of those days. He used the scattered 'islands' of firm ground in the marsh to isolate the dreaded English and Welsh archers and so put them out of range of most of his scratch army.

Battle of Inverlochy (1645)

Montrose's most astonishing victory, against all odds, where he routed much greater Covenant and anti-royalist forces under Argyll by making tremendous forced marches in winter conditions through the West Highland mountains and then using brilliant tactics against a surprised enemy.

Battle of Prestonpans (1745)

Prince Charles Edward's triumph over the Hanoverian army, when his Highland clansmen routed Sir John Cope's professional army by greater mobility and spirit, with Cope having to gallop off the field to reach Coldstream that night, leaving even his military treasure-chest behind with all his cannon and supplies.

214

NIGEL TRANTER'S LIST OF MOST HEROIC DEFEATS

Battle of Dunsinane (1057)

The famous occasion when Birnam Wood came to Dunsinane, as Shakespeare put it, and King MacBeth (a good king and not a bloody tyrant as the play makes out) suffered defeat by Malcolm Canmore, later Malcolm the Third. Malcolm, with largely Northumbrian troops, hit on the notion of using boughs cut from the trees of Birnam Wood to camouflage his army's approach to Dunsinane, which in a scattered-woodland country was successful in surprising the smaller royal force. This hard-fought defeat was the beginning of the end for MacBeth.

Battle of the Standard (or Northallerton) (1138)

David I was one of Scotland's best kings and a peace-maker. This was his only really major battle – and he lost it, during an invasion of England to aid his niece, Queen Maud, to recover her throne from the usurper Stephen. The English army was blessed by the Archbishop of York and given a ship's mast topped by Communion Bread and Wine (the Standard of the battle's name) – and so distressed did the Scots forces become in seeming to fight against the Body and Blood of Christ Himself that their attack failed. It was not a real defeat as the Scots left the field in good order, the English remaining un-moving on their hill; but it was a moral disaster.

Battle of Homildon Hill (1402)

During the weak reign of Robert the Third, the Earl of Douglas led the chivalry of Scotland to utter rout, near Berwick-on-Tweed, by an astonishing disregard for the great fire-power of the English archers, choosing a strong position on Homildon Hill, excellent for defensive warfare but entirely within range of the massed enemy archers, who mowed down the Scots cavalry like corn almost before the latter could come to blows with the English.

Battle of Flodden (1513)

The most famous of all Scottish defeats when James the Fourth led the flower of Scotland to terrible ruin in a too-gallant gesture to aid his French allies, the Queen of France having sent him her glove as a plea. James fought on chivalric lines against the wily Earl of Surrey, who did not, and died in the process, with most of his great army.

Battle of Inverkeithing (1651)

Not very well known but a tragic affair, during Cromwell's campaign to subdue Scotland. His Ironsides, at Inverkeithing in Fife, defeated a Scots force with great slaughter. Refusing to flee, the defenders died where they stood. For instance, there were 800 Macleans there, under their Chief, Sir Hector of Duart. Only 40 survived. Sir Hector fell early and, one after another, seven of his chieftains took his place to die over his body, each shouting 'Another for Hector!'

Battle of Culloden (1746)

The final defeat of the royal Stuart cause, with its heroism and butchery thereafter, too sad for all Scotsmen even now to dwell on once again, so let's have some jokes.

ANDY CAMERON'S TEN QUICK QUIPS

1 'Take away your lochs and mountains and glens and what have you got?' asked the Englishman. 'Easy,' said the Scot. 'England.'

2 What about the Scottish football fan who lost all his luggage on the way to Wembley? The cork fell oot!

3 Angus drove off the first tee at St Andrews. 'Can you see it?' asked his partner. 'See it?' said Angus. 'I can reach it.'

4   The man outside the Rangers Club in Glasgow asked a guy who was leaving the club: 'What's the quickest way to the Royal Infirmary?' 'Away in there,' said the stranger, 'and sing *Danny Boy*.'

5   The American said to the farmer in Fife, 'Back home in the States I've got a ranch and it takes me two days to go round it in my car.' 'Aye,' said the farmer, 'I used to have a car like that.'

6   There was the Glasgow man who asked the doctor for some more sleeping tablets for his wife because she had woken up.

7   Actually, I used to play darts with my wife every week but her head got blunt.

8   Aberdeen is the only city in the world where parents go outside on Christmas Eve and fire a gun – and then go in to tell the kids that somebody has shot Santa Claus.

9   There was the Glasgow man who called his girlfriend Dandruff because she kept falling on his neck.

10 A wee Glasgow guy went into a barber's shop and asked for a Tony Curtis. After the barber had shaved his head, the wee Glaswegian said 'That's no' a Tony Curtis.' 'Aye it is,' said the barber. 'Ah saw him in *The King and I*.'

Wales

POPULATION

1971 census

Total population: 2.7 m (26% Welsh speaking)

Chief cities

Cardiff	278 221
Swansea	172 000
Newport	112 000
Rhondda	88 924

Counties

Clwyd	382 530
Dyfed	325 600
Gwent	435 600
Gwynedd	228 000
Mid Glamorgan	541 700
Powys	108 400
South Glamorgan	396 900
West Glamorgan	364 900

THE TEN HIGHEST WELSH PEAKS

	height in feet
Snowdon	3560
Carnedd Llewelyn	3484
Carnedd Dafydd	3426
Aran Mawddwy	2970
Brecon Beacon	2906
Pen-y-gader fawr	2660
Carmarthen Van	2632
Plinlimmon	2468
Radnor	2163
Drygan Fawr	2155

WELSH COLLIERIES, 1981

National Coal Board

Abernant, near Pontardawe, W Glam. 916 men produce 267 000 tonnes annually

Aberpergwm, Glynneath, W Glam. 322 men, 64 000 tonnes

Abertillery New Mine, Gwent, 896 men, 204 000 tonnes

Bedwas, Trethomas, Gwent. 707 men, 140 000 tonnes

Betws Drift, Ammanford, Dyfed. 569 men, 385 000 tonnes

Blaenant, Crynant, Neath, W Glam. 670 men, 334 000 tonnes

Blaengwrach, Glynneath, W Glam. 268 men, 57 000 tonnes

Blaenserchan, Abersychan, Pontypool, Gwent. 411 men, 73 000 tonnes

Britannia, Pengam, Blackwood, Gwent. 724 men, 181 000 tonnes

Brynlliw/Morlais, Grovesend, Swansea, W Glam. 864 men, 273 000 tonnes

Coegnant, Nantyffyllon, Maesteg, Mid Glam. 509 men, 80 000 tonnes

Cwm/Coedely, Llantwit Fardre, Pontypridd, Mid Glam. 1358 men, 473 000 tonnes

Cwmgwili, Cross Hands, Llanelli, Dyfed. 341 men, 135 000 tonnes

Cynheidre, Five Roads, Llanelli, Dyfed. 1068 men, 205 000 tonnes

Deep Navigation, Treharris, Mid Glam. 774 men, 343 000 tonnes

Garw/Ffaldau, Blaengarw, Bridgend, Mid Glam. 825 men, 225 000 tonnes

Lady Windsor/Abercynon, Ynysybwl, Mid Glam. 1170 men, 312 000 tonnes

Mardy, Rhondda, Mid Glam. 865 men, 200 000 tonnes

Marine, Cwm, Ebbw Vale, Gwent. 591 men, 148 000 tonnes

Markham, Blackwood, Gwent. 565 men, 189 000 tonnes

Merthyr Vale, Mid Glam. 699 men, 246 000 tonnes

Nantgarw/Windsor, Taffs Well, Mid Glam. 613 men, 244 000 tonnes

North Celynen, Newbridge, Gwent. 608 men, 168 000 tonnes

Oakdale, Blackwood, Gwent. 945 men, 226 000 tonnes

Penallta, Hengoed, Mid Glam. 642 men, 192 000 tonnes

Penrikyber, Penrhiwceiber, Mountain Ash, Mid Glam. 754 men, 217 000 tonnes

St John's, Maesteg, Mid Glam. 818 men, 188 000 tonnes

Six Bells, Abertillery, Gwent. 503 men, 115 000 tonnes

South Celynen, Newbridge, Gwent. 488 men, 108 000 tonnes

Taff Merthyr, Trelwis, Treharris, Mid Glam. 643 men, 478 000 tonnes

Tower/Fernhill, Hirwaun, Aberdare, Mid Glam. 811 men, 243 000 tonnes

Treforgan, Crynant, Neath, W Glam. 482 men, 158 000 tonnes

Trelewis Drift, Trelewis, Treharris, Mid Glam. 351 men, 306 000 tonnes

Wyndham/Western, Ogmore Vale, Mid Glam. 914 men, 144 000 tonnes

WELSH WORDS

A quick lesson in Welsh for those who are travelling in Wales and want to understand what on earth the place names are all about. These are the commonest prefixes to place-names, as listed in the book *Welsh Place-Names* by E. M. Davies.

Aber – the mouth of a river or stream
> *Aberystwyth*: mouth of river Ystwyth

Betws – a house of prayer. Its location or name of founder follows
> *Betws-y-coed*: prayer house in the wood

Blaen – the source of a river or the head of a valley
> *Blaenau Ffestiniog*: heads of valleys in the Ffestiniog area

Bwlch – a pass or gap
> *Bwlch y Mynydd*: mountain pass

Capel – chapel
> *Capel Dewi*: the chapel of David

Castell – castle
> *Castell Coch*: red castle

Coed – wood
> *Coed y Brenin*: King's wood

Cwm – valley
> *Cwm Rhondda*: Rhondda valley

Dan – below
> *Dan yr Ogof*: under the cave

Eglwys – church
> *Eglwys y Drindod*: trinity church

Esgair – ridge
> *Esgair Ddu*: black ridge

Ffridd – mountain pasture
> *Ffridd Isaf*: lower mountain pasture

Ffynnon – well or spring
> *Ffynnongroyw*: clear spring

Gelli – grove
> *Gelli Aur*: golden grove

Glan – river bank or shore
    Glanllyn: lakeside
Glyn – valley
    Glynebwy: Ebbw Vale
Gors – bog, fen or marsh
    Gorseinon: marshland in Einon area
Hafod – summer place
    Hafod Wen: fair summer dwelling
Llan – a church
    Llanfairpwllgwyngyllgogerychwyrndrobwll-llantysilio-gogogoch. Church of Saint Mary near the white hazel, near the rapid whirlpool, Church of Saint Tysilio and the red cave.
Llwyn – bush or grove
    Llwyn Onn: Ash grove
Llyn – lake or pool
    Llyn Bala: Bala Lake
Maes – field or plain
    Maesteg: fine field
Moel – bare hill
    Moel Sych: dry bare hill
Mynydd – mountain
    Mynydd Eryri: Snowdon mountain
Nant – stream
    Nantgarw: rough stream
Pant – hollow or valley
    Pantycelyn: hollow of holly trees
Pen – top or end
    Penybont: Bridgend
Pentre – village
    Pentre Bont: village with the bridge
Pont – Bridge
    Pontnewydd: Newbridge
Pwll – pool or pit
    Pwllheli: pool of salt water
Rhiw – slope or hillside
    Rhiwlas: green slope
Rhos – moorland
    Rhosllannerchrugog: moorland of the heathery glade

Rhyd – ford or stream
    Rhydaman: ford over the river Aman
Tal – end or front
    Tal-y-bont: end of the bridge
Tre(f) – homestead or town
    Treherbert: Herbert's homestead
Tŷ – house
    Tyddewi: home of Dewi (St David)
Tyn (short form of Tyddyn) – smallholding
    Tyn-y-pwll: smallholding with a pool
Waun – moorland or meadow
    Waunfawr: large meadow
Ystrad – wide bottomed valley
    Ystradgynlais: Cynlais valley

LLAN SONG

If the printers haven't already gone on strike, let's all try and sing this song. It was found on a yellowed and torn newspaper cutting by Mr E. R. Evans of Anglesey and should be sung to the tune 'Llwyn Onn'. It is in fact a list of all the villages with the prefix Llan (Church of) in Anglesey.

Llandegfan, Llanbeulan, Llanffinian, Llanidan,
Llangwyllog, Llanfwrog, Llanfaelog a'r plas;
Llanddona, Llansadwrn, Llaneugrad, Llanallgo,
A Llanfair yng Nghornwy, ynys Llanddwyn, Llanfaes;
Llanfaethlu, Llanfachreth, Llanrhyddlad, Llangeinwen,
Llanddyfnau, Llangristiolus a Llanerchymedd,
Llanrhwydrus, Llanfechell, a Llanfairmathafarn,
Llanfugail, Llanfflewyn, Llanwenllwyfo bro hedd.

Llanddeusant, Llanddrygarn, Llanddaniel, Llanedwen,
A Llanfairynneubwll, Llandyfrydog, Llangoed,
Llanfihangel-yn-nhowyn a Llanfair-yn-y-cwmwd,

Llangadwaladr, Llanbadrig, Llangefni erioed:
Llanfairpwllgwyngyll, Llaniestyn, Llanllibio,
Llanfihangel-tre'r-beirdd, Llantysilio-gogogoch;
Llanynghenedl, Llangaffo, Llantrisant, Llanbabo,
Llanfihangel-tyn-sylwy a Llanbedrgoch.

OLD-FASHIONED
WELSH FOODS

Cacen grîn – a kind of cake made with flour, sugar, eggs and milk and fried on a griddle.

Posal dŵr – buttermilk mixed with boiling water until it curdles. The curdle goes to the bottom and you drink the remaining liquid. Supposed to be good for colds.

Bara llefrith – bread cut up into a bowl of hot milk.

Bara llaeth – same as before but with buttermilk.

Maidd yr iar – same again but with an egg.

Brwas bara ceirch – home made oatcakes.

Teisen gocos – a kind of cockle omelette made with flour.

Stwnsh rwdan/ffa – mashed potato with swede/beans and buttermilk

Lob Scaws – basically a stew of beef or mutton with onions and carrots.

PRINCES AND PRINCESSES

Welsh Princes of Wales

Independent princes AD 844 to 1282

	reigned
Rhodri the Great	844–878
Anarawd, son of Rhodri	878–916
Hywel Dda, the Good	916–950
Iago ab Idwal (or Ieuaf)	950–979
Hywel ab Ieuaf, the Bad	979–985
Cadwallon, his brother	985–986
Maredudd ab Owain ap Hywel Dda	986–999
Cynan ap Hywel ab Ieuaf	999–1008
Llywelyn ap Sitsyhlt	1008–1023
Iago ab Idwal ap Meurig	1023–1039
Gruffydd ap Llywelyn ap Seisyll	1039–1063
Bleddyn ap Cynfyn	1063–1075
Trahaern ap Caradog	1075–1081
Gruffydd ap Cynan ab Iago	1081–1137
Owain Gwynedd	1137–1170
Dafydd ab Owain Gwynedd	1170–1194
Llywelyn Fawr, the Great	1194–1240
Dafydd ap Llywelyn	1240–1246
Llywelyn ap Gruffydd ap Llywelyn	1246–1282

English Princes of Wales (since AD 1301)

After the conquest of the Welsh by those beastly English, there began a line of English-born Princes of Wales:

Edward, b 1284 (Edward II), cr. Prince of Wales	1301
Edward the Black Prince, son of Edward III	1343
Richard (Richard II) son of the Black Prince	1377
Henry of Monmouth (Henry V)	1399
Edward of Westminster, son of Henry VI	1454
Edward, son of Richard III	1483

Arthur Tudor, son of Henry VII	1489
Henry Tudor (Henry VIII), son of Henry VII	1503
Henry Stuart, son of James I	1610
Charles Stuart (Charles I), son of James I	1616
Charles (Charles II) son of Charles I	1630
James Francis Edward Stuart, 'The Old Pretender'	1688
George Augustus (George II), son of George I	1714
Frederick Lewis, son of George II	1727
George William Frederick (George III)	1751
George Augustus Frederick (George IV)	1762
Albert Edward (Edward VII)	1841
George (George V)	1901
Edward (Edward VIII)	1910
Charles Philip Arthur George	1968

Princesses of Wales

	married to
Joan of Kent (c. 1328–85)	The Black Prince
Anne Neville (1456–85)	Richard II *and* then Edward of Westminster
Catherine of Aragon (1485–1536)	Arthur Tudor *and* then Henry Tudor
Caroline of Bradenburg-Anspach (1683–1737)	George Augustus
Augusta of Saxe-Gotha (1719–72)	Frederick Lewis
Caroline of Brunswick-Wolfenbuttel (1768–1821)	George Augustus Frederick
Alexander of Denmark (1844–1925)	Albert Edward
Mary of Teck (1867–1953)	George
Lady Diana Spencer (b. 1961)	Charles Philip Arthur George

Although there have been twenty Princes of Wales since 1301, there have been only nine Princesses. This is because nine princes died unmarried or married after they had become King; while James 'The Old Pretender' and Edward VIII each married after abdicating.

NAMES

Welsh surnames

Many of Britain's most popular surnames have their highest incidence in and around Cardiff.

name	frequency
Jones (2nd in Britain)	1 in 25 families
Davies (6th)	1 in 30
Williams (3rd)	1 in 35
Thomas (8th)	1 in 45
Evans (7th)	1 in 50
Lewis (19th)	1 in 70
Morgan (37th)	1 in 70
James	1 in 115
Edwards	1 in 130
Griffiths	1 in 130
Price	1 in 140
Phillips	1 in 150
Harris	1 in 175
Morris (28th)	1 in 215

Welsh nicknames

Because everyone in Wales seems to have the same surnames, nicknames have become a necessity. It's often the only way to differentiate between the hundreds of people in the same area all called Davies, Jones, Evans, or Williams. Trevor Fishlock, India correspondent of *The Times*, unearthed many unusual ones during his period as Welsh Affairs Correspondent. Here is a selection, all of them genuine.

Dai Quiet Wedding – was poor and got married in plimsolls.
Dai Death Club – was the man from the insurance.

Dai Piano – was not known for his playing ability, but for cadging cigarettes. His friends would ask 'No cigarettes today, Dai?' 'No, left them home on the piano.'

Jones Balloon – was a foreman who said to his men, 'Don't let me down, boys.'

Mrs Dai Eggs – was married to an egg-seller in Swansea. She gave birth to twins and became Mrs Dai Double-Yolk.

Dai Bananas – was Sir David Maxwell-Fyfe, Minister for Welsh Affairs.

Will Casgen-gwrw – (Will Beerbarrel) – was the man who rolled a barrel of ale to the foundry for the thirsty metalworkers.

Eddie Click Click – was a photographer in Carmarthenshire.

Owen One-I-Got – was a tightfisted man who, whenever he was asked for a sweet or cigarette, invariably had just one left. 'Only one I got,' he would say, putting the packet away.

Exactly Jones – was named after his favourite word.

Jones Caerphilly – always had cheese sandwiches for lunch.

Dai Central 'eating – only had one tooth.

Mrs Thomas Pay Cash – abhorred hire purchase.

Billy Never-never – was a celibate.

Evans the Arrow – Alan Evans, one of the best darts players in the world.

WELSH RAILS

Railway preservation started in Wales with the founding of the Talyllyn Railway Society in 1950. Now there are eight Light Railways in Wales.

1   *Bala Lake Railway (Rheilffordd Llyn Bala)*. Gauge 1ft 11½ins. Distance 4½ miles Llanuwchlyn to Bala Lake, with plans to extend half a mile to reach nearer into Bala town.

2   *Fairbourne Railway*. Gauge 15ins, two miles long; runs from Fairbourne on the Mawddach estuary to the ferry across the estuary to Barmouth.

3   *Festiniog Railway.* Thirteen miles of track 1ft 11½ ins gauge. Runs from Porthmadog on the coast to Ffestiniog.
4   *Llanberis Lake Railway.* Narrow 1ft 11½ ins gauge running the length of Lake Padarn.
5   *Snowdon Mountain Railway,* gauge of 2ft 7½ ins; rack operated, five-mile length up to the summit of Snowdon.
6   *Vale of Rheidol Railway.* Aberystwyth to Devil's Bridge, a distance of 11 miles. It runs on the level for the first five miles, then at a gradient of 1 in 50 for the next seven miles. Gauge is 1ft 11½ ins.
7   *Welshpool and Llanfair Light Railway.* Five and a half miles from Llanfair Caereinion to Welshpool on 2ft 6ins gauge.
8   *Talyllyn Railway.* Seven miles from Tywyn on the coast to Nant Gwernol inland, 2ft 3ins gauge.

WELSH PROS

A few of Wales's current contributors to the entertainment world.

Max Boyce	Sian Phillips
Richard Burton	Shakin' Stevens
Windsor Davies	Tessie O'Shea
Harry Secombe	Tom Jones

RELIGIOUS REVIVALS IN WALES

1   Vicar Pritchard in Llandovery 1620–1630. He helped bring about the publication of the first popular edition of the Bible in Wales
2   Missionary revival of 1790–94, influenced zeitgeist of French revolution
3   Practical Revival 1806–09. John Elias started the idea of Sunday School
4   Christmas Evans's theological and spiritual revival 1814–15
5   Rev John Jones of Talsarn, a celebrated Calvinistic minister, led a quiet revival, 1839–42
6   The Cholera Revival 1849–50. Noted for its fierceness, backsliders and the suddenness with which it lifted after the disappearance of the disease
7   The 1859 Revival, led by Humphrey Jones, 1858–60. He eventually broke down, retired into obscurity and was consigned to a lunatic asylum
8   Evan Roberts in 1904 led a revival which shook all of Wales. It was to be the final death rattle of non-conformity in Wales

UNIVERSITIES

The University of Wales, established 1893
Colleges:
Aberystwyth (2607 undergraduates)
Bangor, North Wales (2331)
Cardiff, Institute of Science and Technology (2483)
Cardiff, National School of Medicine (672)
Cardiff, University College (4478)
Lampeter (St David's College) 687
Swansea (3199)

Other colleges:
Polytechnic of Wales, Pontypridd, Mid Glamorgan
Gwent College of Higher Education, Caerleon, Gwent
College of Librarianship Wales, Aberystwyth
Normal College of Education, Bangor, North Wales
North Wales Institute of Higher Education, Wrexham, Clwyd
South Glamorgan Institute of Higher Education, Cyncoed, Cardiff
Trinity College, Carmarthen, Dyfed
Welsh College of Music and Drama, Cathays Park, Cardiff

NAKED WELSH

With all that religion and education and singing, it's surprising the Welsh have time for any other pleasures, but there's recently been a naturist revival, if a rather unofficial one. If you're looking for nudes in Wales, or feel like stripping off, these are the beaches to head for. On each of them, you can go as naked as nature – if not the local council – intended.

White Beach, Anglesey
Aberffraw, Anglesey
Hell's Mouth, Lleyn Peninsula, Caernarvon
Harlech North
Morfa Dyffryn
Marros Sands, Dyfed
Pembrey Forest
Whitford, Gower Peninsula

HISTORIC WELSH MONUMENTS

Beaumaris Castle, Anglesey, Gwynedd
Caerleon Roman Amphitheatre, Gwent
Caernarvon Castle, Gwynedd
Caerphilly Castle, Glamorgan
Chepstow Castle, Gwent
Conwy Castle, Gwynedd
Criccieth, Gwynedd
Denbigh, Clwyd
Harlech, Gwynedd
Raglan, Gwent
St David's Bishop's Palace, Dyfed
Tintern Abbey, Gwent

WONDERS

Ancient wonders of Wales

Chosen by Wynford Vaughan Thomas, with the help of listeners of Radio Wales's AM programme.

1   Culver Hole, Port Eynon, Gower (a walled-up smuggler's cave into which you crawl through a small hole)
2   Twelve long-drop loos in the walls of Conway Castle
3   Vale of Neath Waterfalls
4   St David's Cathedral
5   Snowdon
6   The Great Cliff, Llyn y Fan Fach, Carmarthen
7   Gogarth Cliff, Holyhead Mountain (biggest cliff-drop in Wales)

Modern wonders of Wales

Chris Stuart, presenter of the AM programme in Wales, asked his listeners what they thought would make up a good list of modern wonders of Wales. This time he wanted topics as well as places.

1 The literature of Wales
2 The Roman goldmine at Dolaucothi, Pembrokeshire
3 The Port Talbot Steelworks
4 Calvinistic Methodist chapel in Llangeitho, Cardiganshire
5 Rhyl sands
6 Pendine sands
7 The Cardiff dialect
8 Gower peninsula
9 A round, communal lavatory on the quayside, Penrhyn Port, near Bangor, North Wales

WELSH MYTHS

Our Welsh editor has gathered twelve popular misconceptions about Wales and the Welsh, all taken from people who've never been there.

1 All sentences contain the words 'Indeed to goodness', 'look you' and 'boyo'.
2 They wear stove-pipe hats.
3 They can all sing beautifully.
4 Most of them are miners and go to chapel on Sundays.
5 Most of them are farmers and go to sheep dog trials on Saturdays.
6 They eat leeks with, and in, everything – leek soup, leek pie, leek ratatouille.
7 They talk a lot, drink a lot and tell tall stories.
8 An immoral lot, but must be seen to be upstanding and upright.
9 They are all a bit clannish – and smug with it – exemplified by Clive Jenkins's voice.

10 Well-educated, and terribly snobbish about the professions.
11 They're all dark, small and swarthy.
12 Everybody knows everybody else.

NON-FICTION

GENERAL
- [ ] The Chinese Mafia — Fenton Bresler — £1.50
- [ ] The Piracy Business — Barbara Conway — £1.50
- [ ] Strange Deaths — John Dunning — £1.35
- [ ] Shocktrauma — John Franklin & Alan Doelp — £1.50
- [ ] The War Machine — James Avery Joyce — £1.50

BIOGRAPHY/AUTOBIOGRAPHY
- [ ] All You Needed Was Love — John Blake — £1.50
- [ ] Clues to the Unknown — Robert Cracknell — £1.50
- [ ] William Wordsworth — Hunter Davies — £1.95
- [ ] The Family Story — Lord Denning — £1.95
- [ ] The Borgias — Harry Edgington — £1.50
- [ ] Rachman — Shirley Green — £1.50
- [ ] Nancy Astor — John Grigg — £2.95
- [ ] Monty: The Making of a General 1887-1942 — Nigel Hamilton — £4.95
- [ ] The Windsors in Exile — Michael Pye — £1.50
- [ ] 50 Years with Mountbatten — Charles Smith — £1.25
- [ ] Maria Callas — Arianna Stassinopoulos — £1.75
- [ ] Swanson on Swanson — Gloria Swanson — £2.50

HEALTH/SELF-HELP
- [ ] The Hamlyn Family First Aid Book — Dr Robert Andrew — £1.50
- [ ] Girl! — Brandenburger & Curry — £1.25
- [ ] The Good Health Guide for Women — Cooke & Dworkin — £2.95
- [ ] The Babysitter Book — Curry & Cunningham — £1.25
- [ ] Living Together — Dyer & Berlins — £1.50
- [x] The Pick of Woman's Own Diets — Jo Foley — 95p
- [ ] Coping With Redundancy — Fred Kemp — £1.50
- [ ] Cystitis: A Complete Self-help Guide — Angela Kilmartin — £1.00
- [ ] Fit for Life — Donald Norfolk — £1.35
- [ ] The Stress Factor — Donald Norfolk — £1.25
- [ ] Fat is a Feminist Issue — Susie Orbach — £1.25
- [ ] Fat is a Feminist Issue II — Susie Orbach — £3.50
- [ ] Living With Your New Baby — Rakowitz & Rubin — £1.50
- [ ] Related to Sex — Claire Rayner — £1.50
- [ ] Natural Sex — Mary Shivanandan — £1.25
- [ ] Woman's Own Birth Control — Dr Michael Smith — £1.25
- [ ] Overcoming Depression — Dr Andrew Stanway — £1.50
- [ ] Health Shock — Martin Weitz — £1.75

POCKET HEALTH GUIDES
- [ ] Depression and Anxiety — Dr Arthur Graham — 85p
- [ ] Diabetes — Dr Alex D. G. Gunn — 85p
- [ ] Heart Trouble — Dr Simon Joseph — 85p
- [ ] High Blood Pressure — Dr James Knapton — 85p
- [ ] The Menopause — Studd & Thom — 85p
- [ ] Children's Illnesses — Dr Luke Zander — 85p

TRAVEL
- [ ] The Complete Traveller — Joan Bakewell — £1.95
- [ ] Time Out London Shopping Guide — Lindsey Bareham — £1.50
- [ ] A Walk Around the Lakes — Hunter Davies — £1.75
- [ ] Britain By Train — Patrick Goldring — £1.75
- [ ] England By Bus — Elizabeth Gundrey — £1.25
- [ ] Staying Off the Beaten Track — Elizabeth Gundrey — £2.95
- [ ] Britain at Your Feet — Wickers & Pedersen — £1.75

HUMOUR
- [ ] Don't Quote Me — Atyeo & Green — £1.00
- [ ] Ireland Strikes Back! — Seamus B. Gorrah — 85p
- [ ] Pun Fun — Paul Jennings — 95p
- [ ] 1001 Logical Laws — John Peers — 95p
- [ ] The Devil's Bedside Book — Leonard Rossiter — 85p

REFERENCE

- ☐ The Sunday Times Guide to
  Movies on Television   Angela & Elkan Allan   £1.50
- ☐ The Cheiro Book of Fate and Fortune   £1.50
- ☐ Hunter Davies's Book of British Lists   £1.25
- ☐ NME Guide to Rock Cinema   Fred Dellar   £1.50
- ☐ What's Wrong With Your Pet?   Hugo Kerr   95p
- ☐ The Drinker's Companion   Derek Nimmo   £1.25
- ☐ The Complete Book of Cleaning   Barty Phillips   £1.50
- ☐ The Oscar Movies from A-Z   Roy Pickard   £1.25
- ☐ Collecting For Profit   Sam Richards   £1.25
- ☐ Islam   D. S. Roberts   £1.50
- ☐ Questions of Motoring Law   John Spencer   £1.25
- ☐ Questions of Law   Bill Thomas   £1.25

GAMES AND PASTIMES

- ☐ The Hamlyn Book of Wordways 1   75p
- ☐ The Hamlyn Family Quiz Book   85p

WAR

- ☐ The Battle of Malta   Joseph Attard   £1.50
- ☐ World War 3   Edited by Shelford Bidwell   £1.50
- ☐ The Black Angels   Rupert Butler   £1.35
- ☐ Gestapo   Rupert Butler   £1.50
- ☐ Hand of Steel   Rupert Butler   £1.35
- ☐ The Flight of the Mew Gull   Alex Henshaw   £1.75
- ☐ Sigh for a Merlin   Alex Henshaw   £1.50
- ☐ Hitler's Secret Life   Glenn B. Infield   £1.25

GARDENING

- ☐ 'Jock' Davidson's House Plant Book   £1.50
- ☐ A Vegetable Plot for Two — or More   D. B. Clay Jones   £1.00
- ☐ Salads the Year Round   Joy Larkcom   £1.50
- ☐ Gardening Tips of A Lifetime   Fred Loads   £1.50
- ☐ Sunday Telegraph Patio Gardening   Robert Pearson   £1.00
- ☐ Greenhouse Gardening   Sue Phillips   £1.25

COOKERY

- ☐ A-Z of Health Foods   Carol Bowen   £1.50
- ☐ The Giant Sandwich Book   Carol Bowen   £1.50
- ☐ Vegetarian Cookbook   Dave Dutton   £1.50
- ☐ Jewish Cookbook   Florence Greenberg   £1.50
- ☐ Know Your Onions   Kate Hastrop   95p
- ☐ Indian Cooking   Attia Hosain and Sita Pasricha   £1.50
- ☐ Home Preserving and Bottling   Gladys Mann   80p
- ☐ Home Baked Breads & Cakes   Mary Norwak   75p
- ☐ Easy Icing   Marguerite Patten   85p
- ☐ Wine Making At Home   Francis Pinnegar   80p
- ☐ Cooking for Christmas   Shona Crawford Poole   £1.50
- ☐ Microwave Cookbook   Jill Spencer   £1.25
- ☐ Mixer and Blender Cookbook   Myra Street   80p
- ☐ Diabetic Cookbook   Elisabeth Russell Taylor   £1.50
- ☐ The Hamlyn Pressure Cookbook   Jane Todd   85p

HUMOUR

- ☐ Don't Quote Me   Atyeo & Green   £1.00
- ☐ Ireland Strikes Back!   Seamus B. Gorrah   85p
- ☐ Pun Fun   Paul Jennings   95p
- ☐ 1001 Logical Laws   John Peers   95p
- ☐ The Devil's Bedside Book   Leonard Rossiter   85p

FICTION

GENERAL

☐ Chains	Justin Adams	£1.25
☐ Secrets	F. Lee Bailey	£1.25
☐ Skyship	John Brosnan	£1.65
☐ The Free Fishers	John Buchan	£1.50
☐ Huntingtower	John Buchan	£1.50
☐ Midwinter	John Buchan	£1.25
☐ A Prince of the Captivity	John Buchan	£1.25
☐ The Eve of St Venus	Anthony Burgess	£1.10
☐ Nothing Like the Sun	Anthony Burgess	£1.50
☐ The Memoirs of Maria Brown	John Cleland	£1.25
☐ The Last Liberator	John Clive	£1.25
☐ Wyndward Fury	Norman Daniels	£1.50
☐ Ladies in Waiting	Gwen Davis	£1.50
☐ The Money Wolves	Paul Erikson	£1.50
☐ Rich Little Poor Girl	Terence Feely	£1.50
☐ Fever Pitch	Betty Ferm	£1.50
☐ The Bride of Lowther Fell	Margaret Forster	£1.75
☐ Forced Feedings	Maxine Herman	£1.50
☐ Savannah Blue	William Harrison	£1.50
☐ Duncton Wood	William Horwood	£1.95
☐ Dingley Falls	Michael Malone	£1.95
☐ Gossip	Marc Olden	£1.25
☐ Buccaneer	Dudley Pope	£1.50
☐ An Inch of Fortune	Simon Raven	£1.25
☐ The Dream Makers	John Sherlock	£1.50
☐ The Reichling Affair	Jack Stoneley	£1.75
☐ Eclipse	Margaret Tabor	£1.35
☐ Pillars of the Establishment	Alexander Thynn	£1.50
☐ Cat Stories	Stella Whitelaw	£1.10

WESTERN — BLADE SERIES by Matt Chisholm

☐ No. 5 The Colorado Virgins	85p
☐ No. 6 The Mexican Proposition	85p
☐ No. 7 The Arizona Climax	85p
☐ No. 8 The Nevada Mustang	85p
☐ No. 9 The Montana Deadlock	95p
☐ No. 10 The Cheyenne Trap	95p
☐ No. 11 The Navaho Trail	95p
☐ No. 12 The Last Act	95p

WESTERN — McALLISTER SERIES by Matt Chisholm

☐ McAllister and the Spanish Gold	95p
☐ McAllister on the Commanche Crossing	95p
☐ McAllister Never Surrenders	95p
☐ McAllister and the Cheyenne Trap	95p

SCIENCE FICTION

☐ Times Without Number	John Brunner	£1.10
☐ The Dancers of Arun	Elizabeth A. Lynn	£1.50
☐ Watchtower	Elizabeth A. Lynn	£1.10

WAR

☐ The Andersen Assault	Peter Leslie	£1.25
☐ Killers under a Cruel Sky	Peter Leslie	£1.25
☐ The Serbian Triangle	Peter Saunders	£1.10
☐ Jenny's War	Jack Stoneley	£1.25

FICTION

CRIME/ADVENTURE/SUSPENSE

☐ The Killing In The Market	John Ball with Bevan Smith	£1.00
☐ In the Heat of the Night	John Ball	£1.00
☐ Johnny Get Your Gun	John Ball	£1.00
☐ The Cool Cottontail	John Ball	£1.00
☐ The Megawind Cancellation	Bernard Boucher	£1.25
☐ Tunnel	Hal Friedman	£1.35
☐ Tagget	Irving A. Greenfield	£1.25
☐ Don't be no Hero	Leonard Harris	£1.25
☐ The Blunderer	Patricia Highsmith	£1.25
☐ A Game for the Living	Patricia Highsmith	£1.25
☐ Those Who Walk Away	Patricia Highsmith	£1.25
☐ The Tremor of Forgery	Patricia Highsmith	£1.25
☐ The Two Faces of January	Patricia Highsmith	£1.25
☐ Labyrinth	Eric Mackenzie-Lamb	£1.25
☐ The Hunted	Elmore Leonard	£1.25
☐ The Traitor Machine	Max Marquis	£1.25
☐ The Triad Imperative	Dwight Martin	£1.50
☐ Confess, Fletch	Gregory Mcdonald	90p
☐ Fletch	Gregory Mcdonald	90p
☐ Fletch's Fortune	Gregory Mcdonald	£1.25
☐ Flynn	Gregory Mcdonald	95p
☐ All the Queen's Men	Guiy de Montfort	£1.25
☐ Pandora Man	Newcomb & Schaefer	£1.25
☐ Skyfire	Thomas Page	£1.50
☐ The Last Prisoner	James Robson	£1.50
☐ The Croesus Conspiracy	Ben Stein	£1.25
☐ Deadline in Jakarta	Ian Stewart	£1.25
☐ The Seizing of Singapore	Ian Stewart	£1.00
☐ The Earhart Betrayal	James Stewart Thayer	£1.50

HISTORICAL ROMANCE/ROMANCE/SAGA

☐ Hawksmoor	Aileen Armitage	£1.75
☐ Pipistrelle	Aileen Armitage	£1.25
☐ Blaze of Passion	Stephanie Blake	£1.25
☐·Daughter of Destiny	Stephanie Blake	£1.50
☐ Flowers of Fire	Stephanie Blake	£1.50
☐ So Wicked My Desire	Stephanie Blake	£1.50
☐ Unholy Desires	Stephanie Blake	£1.50
☐ Wicked is My Flesh	Stephanie Blake	£1.50
☐ Lovers and Dancers	Michael Feeney Callan	£1.50
☐ The Far Morning	Brenda Clarke	£1.50

NAME ....

ADDRESS ....

....

Write to Hamlyn Paperbacks Cash Sales, PO Box 11, Falmouth, Cornwall TR10 9EN.

Please indicate order and enclose remittance to the value of the cover price plus:

U.K.: Please allow 45p for the first book plus 20p for the second book and 14p for each additional book ordered, to a maximum charge of £1.63.

B.F.P.O. & EIRE: Please allow 45p for the first book plus 20p for the second book and 14p per copy for the next 7 books, thereafter 8p per book.

OVERSEAS: Please allow 75p for the first book and 21p per copy for each additional book.

Whilst every effort is made to keep prices low it is sometimes necessary to increase cover prices and also postage and packing rates at short notice. Hamlyn Paperbacks reserve the right to show new retail prices on covers which may differ from those previously advertised in the text or elsewhere.